The Second Battle of Hastings

By

Charles Eldridge

The Second Battle of Hastings

A CIP catalogue record for this book
is available from the British Library.

ISBN 0-9547279-0-8

Published by Charles Eldridge.

2004

Foreword

Charles Eldridge has lived all his life on The Ridge at Hastings. Born in 1927, he has seen Baldslow change from a quiet Village to the over-burdened road junction it is today. Seeing the war years through the eyes of a boy, he has always wondered, "What if the German Army had landed?" In this book he has imagined how it might have been, making a robust story with a hint of romance.

Acknowledgements

I acknowledge with grateful thanks the help and encouragement given to me by my wife Enid M. Eldridge in the production of this book. I particularly mention the watercolour illustrations painted by her. The sketches for these are based on old photographs, which she has skilfully brought to life, to give the reader a sense of the atmosphere in which the story takes place.

Grateful thanks also go to my daughter Joanna, who typed and retyped the script, and to Alan Buckle. Colin and Mary Eldridge, and to Joyce Harris who have all given me valuable help and advice.

.

Author's Note

Literary works fall into various categories. They can be Fact (which is usually called Non-Fiction and embraces History, Biography, Science, etc.). There is Fiction, where stories spring from the writer's imagination, mostly romance and adventure and there is what is called Faction, where a true story is enlarged and embroidered to introduce fictitious characters to make is more interesting.

This story does not fall easily into any of these. The basis is well known fact. The fall of France and the evacuation of Dunkirk, left Britain undefeated, yet, for some months, virtually defenceless against invasion. In the late Summer of 1940 it would have been easier for an enemy landing on the south-east coast to march to London than at any time in history. And yet it did not happen. The German Air Chief, Goering, said that his Luftwaffe on its own would bring Britain to its knees, but the R.A.F. was holding them and the tide was turning. It was now or never for Hitler. It was for him to make the decision. His Army Chiefs were pressing for action, yet he could not make up his mind. Why he did not give the order to invade we shall never know.

This much is fact and can be found in history books and War records. It is from this scenario that my story springs, and from that point on, it is pure imagination. I have brought in some characters whom I knew well, and used the names of

others who have an association with the district. I trust that after 60 years this will cause no-one any distress.

The story is serious. War is not funny, and I have made no attempt to bring humour into it. I hope it will provoke interest and, perhaps deeper thoughts. I know it could have happened, but as it is all from my imagination, I have called it....

A FANTASY.

Preface

The early morning air was filled with the noise of aircraft engines. The big Junkers troop carriers released the towing hawsers of the gliders and headed back across the Channel as quickly as they could to avoid interception. The gliders silently approached their chosen landing ground. The invasion of England had begun!

Chapter 1

A volley of shots rang out, shattering the peace of the Summer morning. An old man who was walking down the road past the farm dropped to his knees and looked around for shelter. I called out to him,

"Don't be alarmed Sir, it's only my sons practicing for the clay pigeon shoot."

He looked relieved and continued his walk towards me. I studied him as he approached. Despite his age and lameness, he could still stand upright with an almost military bearing.

"Good Morning," he said.

I had been cutting the hedge beside my farm gate, so I put my tools in my barrow to give him my full attention.

"Is this your farm and have you lived here long?" His English was good and yet he was quite certainly foreign.

He continued, "I have not been here for very many years, but I remember a little Church made of iron which I thought was here, can you direct me to it?"

I realised now that his accent was continental, most probably German. His tone was quite genuine, and I found myself intrigued by his question and wishing to help him.

"Yes, there was an iron church right here, and we are standing just where its doorway was, but come into the farm entrance away from the traffic and, perhaps I can tell you more."

He seemed pleased at my friendly response, and we moved together through the farm gate.

"The church was taken down to make way for widening the road," I said, "We lost our old house too, and had to build a new one." then, as an afterthought, I said, "I have the old church bell in that bell tower in my garden."

"And can you still ring it?" he asked, "and does it still sound the same?"

"Oh yes," I said, "Would you like to hear it?"

His eyes lit up.

"Oh please." he said, "I shall remember the sound of that bell to my dying Day. I never thought I should hear it again!"

We moved down the slope towards the garden. Fortunately I had recently trimmed the Clematis Montana which regularly covered the tower, and the bell swung freely. I pulled the cord once and then again and again and the strident, tinny chime rang out over the garden and beyond. I rang it about twenty times as the old man stood almost transfixed and a far-away look came into his eyes. There was a long silence, then, "Thank-you, thank-you," he said, "That brings it all back to me as nothing else possibly could."

"Brings what back? "I said, "Perhaps you would like to come in and have a cup of coffee and tell me all about it?"

"Do not ask me in until you know who I am," he said, "because I might not be welcome. My name is Hans Dietrich Von Muller, and I was last here under very different circumstances. The date was 21st September 1940 and I was a Major in the German Army- I was your enemy!"

There was a moments pause as our eyes met, and I saw in his a longing that a new-found friendship might not be rebuffed as soon as it had begun. I held out my hand.

"Come in," I said, "Nearly sixty years have passed and we are talking of history. Come in, let us be friends and re-live that day together."

And so it was that we sat in easy chairs with a cup of coffee each on the table, while he unfolded for me the story of the day which has become known as 'The Second Battle of Hastings' - a day which went a long way towards swaying the balance of the war.

Chapter 2

Hans settled back in his chair. "I am here on a sentimental journey" he said, "Almost a pilgrimage you might say, but I'll tell you about that later. I think I had better begin at the beginning and tell you a bit about myself. I was born just after the 1914 war had ended and when I was young Germany was a very dull place for a boy. Then in the 1930s came Hitler and, for me, camps. All the while we were told that the peace treaties were unjust, and that one day Germany would be great again. The only aircraft we were allowed were gliders, and soon glider schools were established. I volunteered to attend a course and soon became a qualified pilot."

"How was it that Germany was allowed to re-arm?" I asked.

"It was not difficult. After the armies of occupation were withdrawn, and France and Britain demobilised, the groundwork for a new Wermacht and Luftwaffe were quickly established. We all thought that sooner or later there would be another war, and that this time, we should win. The inspiring speeches of Hitler rang in our ears, and we joined the armed forces willingly, almost looking forward to going into battle."

"Where did you do your training?" I enquired.

"Mostly well away from populated areas, as Hitler did not wish to advertise our growing strength, which might cause other countries to re-arm. Churchill warned the British people, but he was out of favour and largely disregarded."

Hans paused to take a sip of his coffee. "Am I boring you?" he asked. "Have you heard all this before?"

"I know the historical facts," I replied, "but it is much more interesting coming from someone who was there. Where were you when the war broke out?"

"In reserve for the troops invading Poland, but we were not required. My glider pilot's certificate had been acknowledged, and I had been sent to detachment training for a new form of warfare - Troop carrying Gliders landing forces behind enemy lines. We heard of the success of our armies in Poland and their rapid victory, but than everything went quiet again. When we invaded Poland, Britain and France had declared war on us, but they were not ready to fight, so preparation continued on both sides, and we felt sure that the Summer of 1940 would bring the battle we longed for."

"I remember that," I said. "some friends of mine were in the B.E.F., and were sent to France in 1939. Everyone thought there would be a re-run of the Flanders battles."

Hans considered for a moment, "That may have been so for you, but Hitler and his generals had planned a blitzkrieg, and we had the mobile forces and air-power to deliver a knock-out punch. On 9th April, German troops marched into Denmark and Norway, meeting little resistance. Then on 10th May came the day we were waiting for!"

"That was the day that Hitler gave the order to invade Belgium and Holland wasn't it? I asked. "What part did you play in that?"

He leaned forward in his chair and his face became quite animated.

"It was a hammer-blow," he said, "and our glider forces were the hammer head. The Belgians had three big forts at Eban-Emael, which they said were impregnable - great underground defences with concrete tops, with the ground cleared in front so that their guns could command the frontier, but we landed our gliders on top of the forts and dropped explosives down the ventilating shafts. They surrendered and the way into Belgium was opened."

The excitement of his recollections seemed to tire him for a moment. "Were you in action after that?" I asked. "No." he replied. "Events moved so swiftly. Our armoured columns swept on, crushing defences and surrounding armies. The Belgians and French surrendered and the British were hemmed in at the Channel ports. Hitler thought our Columns overstretched, so he called a halt. Even our Generals thought this was a mistake, as we had the power to capture them all, but as you know, they escaped from Dunkirk although they left their guns and tanks behind."

"All this is in the history books," I said. "What fascinates me is what came next, and what part you played in it. Where were you when the battles in France died down?"

Hans spent a moment or two in thought. "Yes, it's in the history books," he said, "but I went over it all to show you where I was at the beginning of July in 1940, and how and why I was there."

The conversation we were having gave me a chance to study Hans as he spoke. He seemed a man of certain nobility, perhaps deriving from an aristocratic background. It was easy to imagine him a strong character, firmly in control of his men. Now he had mellowed, his face was lined with the pain of his experiences both in the war and after. He knew that all that was behind him, and yet, through the careworn expression, there still showed a yearning. A feeling that he still had some mission to fulfill.

Chapter 3

It was a nice day and the weather was warm. We moved into the garden and sat on a seat overlooking the country towards Rye. Hans' eyes were thoughtful as he looked over the field towards Hydneye. "It's nice to sit here in peace," he said, "The last time I was here the bullets were flying." I thought he was going to tell me about it, because I was itching to hear, but his mind went back to the original subject.

"When the fighting in France was over, I was stationed at the mouth of the Somme. There was a squadron of JU87 Stuka dive-bombers and a squadron of ME110 long-range fighters. I think they found our Grouppe of six gliders room in a corner because they didn't know what to do with us, or how we would be used. The airfield was quite busy, especially when Reich-Marshal Goering launched his air attacks on British fighter stations in July and August. He boasted that his air force alone would win the war, but we were not so sure. There seemed to be a lot of our planes miss-ing or returning badly damaged. We felt sure that sooner or later the invasion of South-East England must come, and that would be our opportunity."

"I expect it was pretty boring, sitting around doing nothing," I said. "Not really," said Hans, "We had training exercises with the Storm Troops of Army Group A, who were to be our assault group, and, in quieter periods, they sent in some old JU52s for glider tugs, so that we could practise precision landings. Towards the end of August, there were strong rumours that something would happen in September, and we hoped that we should be chosen to be part of it."

I thought of my own boyhood in 1940, and how I had searched the skies for JU52s that might herald an approaching invasion.

"How soon did you hear anything definite?" I asked.

"That came early in September, when I was ordered to join a group of senior officers at the Wermacht H.Q. in Amiens. There had been a meeting at the highest level between Hitler and his Chiefs of Staff, Von Brauchitsch for the Army, Goering for the Airforce and Raeder for the Navy to consider plans for 'Sealion', the invasion of England. Hitler had been unwilling to commit him-self, but had eventually agreed that a 'Reconnaissance in force' should be attempted to test the defence. If a weakness were found, then a stronger blow would follow. He had ordered the Chiefs of Staff to make a suitable plan. remarking as he left the meeting that, as the last successful invasion had been at Hastings, it would be a good psychological move to land there again!"

I was surprised, "Surely you weren't in on such a high level meeting?" "Oh no," said Hans, "Nor any of the other planned meetings. We were just told that there was to be a sudden strike by a small group to capture and hold a stratgetic bridge and road junction. If it was successful then reinforcements would be sent and a full-scale invasion would follow. If not, the assault force would be evacuated by sea shortly afterwards."

"So you started on your assault plans?"

"No we couldn't do that until we knew the target, and that would not be chosen until the latest reconnaissance photographs had been studied. We heard that our twelve gliders would be used, with parachute troops to secure the landing ground. A group of landing craft was to carry the main force, with a submarine and E boats to protect them. Of course the skies would be cleared by Goering's Luftwaffe. There must be absolute secrecy, so that the attack would come as a complete surprise!"

I thought for a moment. "There can only have been a few days in September when the moon and the tides would be favourable?"

"That is so, but any time between 19th and 26th would have done. The weather was another factor, because good visibility would be essential. Even if the British suspected a possible attack, they could not know exactly when it would come." Hans was tired by the talking. The sun was warm and he settled back in his seat and dropped asleep.

Chapter 4

Major Norton sat in his office at Claremont School and reviewed the situation. He was a professional soldier who had fought in the trenches in the Great War. Though due for retirement, he had been retained by his regiment because of the seriousness of the situation. He was under no illusions about the precariousness of the position. He had no heavy weapons, no armour, and the sketchiest of prepared defences. If there were an invasion he would be up against crack Storm Troopers of the German Army. There was one factor in his favour, the Germans would be fighting on foreign soil. His men would be defending the country they loved.

After the School at Ebdens Hill, Baldslow, had been evacuated in early Summer, the buildings had been requisitioned by the Army. The same thing had happened at Hydneye House School on the Ridge, and divided between these two establishments, he had a company of 100 men of the Royal Sussex regiment. They were fine fighting men who had acquitted themselves well in France until ordered to withdraw, leaving their heavy weapons behind. All they had to fight with now, were rifles, grenades and a few light machine guns.

The Battle of Britain was raging overhead, and the previous Sunday had seen the heaviest air battles yet between the RAF and the Luftwaffe. 184 German aircraft were claimed to have been destroyed. It was a great victory, and the tide of the battle seemed to be turning in Britain's favour. The evacuation of the British forces from Dunkirk was being represented as a glorious withdrawal instead of an ignominious defeat, and few people realised how desperate the situation was. The army had to be re-grouped, re-trained, and re-equipped, and, until that could be done, Britain's shores were very vulnerable to an invader. It was decided to defend strategic positions with small companies of men billeted locally, and mobile columns of such armoured vehicles as were available as a strategic reserve inland.

The Major looked at his written orders. He was required to defend Baldslow Village and hold the Harrow Bridge against any attack until the mobile armoured column arrived from its base at Tonbridge. The bridge was to be kept intact as long as possible, to allow a counter attack to pass through to drive the enemy back to the sea. Civilian workers had constructed defence works and there was a ring of 'dragons teeth' round the village, and a 'pill-box' on the road bank opposite the Forge. A window had been knocked through the upstairs wall of the Post Office overlooking the road up the hill, so that a heavy machine gun installed there could command the approach from the East. All the roads had had sockets dug into them so that steel uprights could be quickly installed to form a barrier, 45-gallon drums of petrol had been dug into the road banks at the bridge approaches, and a 500-gallon tank beside the bridge itself. These would be ruptured and ignit-ed if enemy troops got near, creating a sea of flame. Claremont and Hydneye had barricades on the sides away from the road, made of three rolls of concertina barbed wire, two side by side with one on top. The one at Hydneye was extended towards the village across the fields from Beaulieu Farm.

What else could he do? In the last few days, he had sent some men out to dig slit trenches on the tops of the banks by the bridge, and also round the perimeter of Claremont and Hydneye. Another squad was detailed to fill sandbags and build them up round the walls of the Harrow Inn. This would be a fortified Command Centre. He also had to decide how to incorporate the platoon of local Home Guard into his command. They numbered about 20 and were led by Sergeant William Manston who lived in Robertson Terrace adjacent to the Inn. After some thought, he sent them to man the pill-box up the hill, and the Post Office where the 1914-18 war Vickers machine-gun was in place. Now, all he could do, was play a waiting game and try to keep his men alert.

Sister Sarah, a Nun of the Order of the Community of the Holy Family on the Ridge at Baldslow was busy. Sister Sarah was always busy. She was that sort of person. Formerly a nursing Sister in a busy hospital, she found the contemplative life of a Religious Order irksome. The Convent of Holmhurst St Mary was normally home to a girl's boarding school in which many of the Sisters were teachers. The school had been evacuated in July to the Forest of Dean, leaving the buildings empty with only the non-teaching Sisters in residence. Sister Sarah was not an easy person to know, or to get on with. She was a buoyant, domineering character who never let her private thoughts show through. There was no arguing with her, and what she ordered had to be obeyed. Her experiences as a Hospital Sister had given her a hardness, a carapace which served her well when dealing with awkward situations. And yet there must have been a more gentle compassionate side to her, for which her patients had come to be thankful. Sometimes, in an unguarded moment, she would sigh as if she might be recalling some other gentler time in her life, and opportunities which had passed her by. Sister Sarah was great organiser with seemingly inexhaustible energy. The Convent had a Hospice; built in earlier days to house travellers for the night, and still used by the Convent as a visitor's house. When the war broke out, Baldslow Village needed a First Aid point, and she persuaded the Reverend Mother to let the Hospice be used for this purpose. She set about organising it and extra beds were installed. She obtained medical supplies and trained local ladies in First Aid. She even enrolled the Convent Chaplain, Father White as a stretcher-bearer.

With the fall of France and the danger of invasion, Sister Sarah's scope widened. The Home Guard wanted a Casualty Collecting Centre, and, once again, she persuaded the Reverend Mother to let her use the Convent Chapel and Library and convert them into hospital wards. Two local doctors were appointed and more trainee nurses found. She organised exercises to deal with sup-

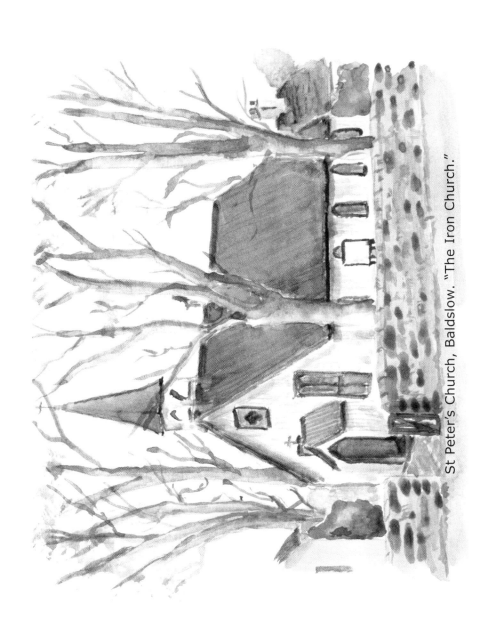

St Peter's Church, Baldslow. "The Iron Church."

A Bren Gun Carrier. Hydneye House in Background

The Ridge. Looking East from Middle Lodge.

The Ridge. Looking East past Beaulieu Farm entrance and Church.

The Ridge. Looking West from St Anne's Gate.

The Ridge, looking West at top of hill. Baldslow Mill on Right.

posed incidents, and local children were pressed into service as 'casualties'. When money for medical supplies ran short, she raised more by organising local people to perform variety shows and pantomimes in the Church Hall, which she produced. All this needed a special release from attending the Convent's daily services, but she welcomed that, as she had found her vocation and she was happy! No-one knew much about her, but there were stories about a tragedy in her younger days which had persuaded her to take up the Convent Life to which she was so ill suited. There was no doubt however of her nursing ability, and in September 1940, the F.A.P. and casualty Collecting Centre stood ready for immediate use.

Chapter 5

Wednesday, 18th September was a bright, clear day with good conditions for flying. The ME110 photo-reconnaissance plane had taken off just before noon for a flight over the south coast of England between Dungeness and Beachy Head. With the RAF fully occupied in fending off the German attacks, it was not intercepted, and taxied in at Abbeville after an uneventful flight. The canisters of film were developed quickly and rushed off to Amiens where the German Chiefs of Staff were meeting. Army Chief Halder was joined by Jeshonek (Airforce) and Schniewind (Navy). They had co-opted Kesselring, the commander of Luftwaffe 2, and Busch of 16th Army Group. Halder addressed the meeting.

"This is a combined operation of a kind which we have not attempted before. Following Hitler's suggestion, it has been decided that Hastings shall be the target, and, subject to weather conditions being favourable, the attack will be made in the early hours of Saturday, 21st September. The objective is to capture the Harrow bridge, an important road junction, 3miles inland, in an assault by air-borne forces, and to hold it until a sea-borne force can be landed and penetrate north to join the air troops. The bridge is to be held for possible reinforcements to penetrate inland. If this operation is not successfully completed by 10am, it will aborted and the attacking force will withdraw by sea. As you know, our greatest advantage will be surprise, so this initial attack will be by a small but powerful group. This will minimise the chance of the plans leaking out beforehand."

Halder paused and leaned back in his chair.

"I think we should check now the forces at our disposal, Navy first please." Schniewind consulted his paper, "I have three fast landing craft at Dieppe disguised as coastal barges. Two of these will each carry three armoured cars and their crews, and the third, two personnel carriers with twenty storm troopers and equipment They will be protected in the crossing by six E boats from Le Havre. A U boat will surface off Hastings and send frogmen ashore in an inflatable dinghy to clear any obstructions on the beach.

Jeshonek spoke next for the Airforce.

"I have two JU52 transport aircraft equipped to carry parachute troops, and twelve more to act as glider tugs. A squadron of Stuka dive bombers will stand by, and fighter cover will be available at first light."

Halder then turned to Busch who said that the necessary para-troops and stormtroopers were in training and were immediately available. He then asked for the latest aerial photos to be laid on the table, and these were keenly studied.

"We shall use these two landing grounds," he said. "The first is the sports ground by the school on the Ridge road, and the second the recreation field to the south of the Village. Troops land-ing on the first will approach the bridge by the Ridge road to secure the top of the bridge, and the second via the main road to take the base. These photos show that defence works are primi-tive, and there are no armoured columns in the area.

Thinking the meeting was ended the officers rose to go, but Halder called them back.

"Good timing is essential," he said, "Sunrise on Saturday, 21st. September will be at 6.42am. The moon is in the third quarter, so there will be some light even before dawn. The paratroops will jump at 5am and prepare the ground for the gliders to land half an hour later. The landing craft will go ashore at first light. I would remind all officers and men that secrecy is our greatest weapon. There must be total surprise!" He added, "I know that the code name for the invasion of England is 'Sea Lion', but the code for our limited operation will be 'Norman Conquest'." The officers left quickly then to meet their own staffs and make their final plans.

Chapter 6

Bletchley Park at Milton Keynes in Buckinghamshire was a very busy place. Situated in an old manor house, it had been secretly developed into the Intelligence Service's centre to intercepting and de-coding the enemy's military communications. The best mathematical and linguistic brains in the country had been assembled, and together they had cracked the code of the 'Enigma' machine. The Germans used this to transmit their orders from Headquarters to army, navy and airforce groups throughout Europe and at sea. Some of the brightest young men and women in the services listened in to this constant stream of messages, and from them tried to assess when and where the next aggressive move would come.

It was known that the code name, 'Sea Lion' meant the invasion of England, and this was heard more and more in September. It became known that landing barges were being assembled in Holland and the Channel ports, and that military units were on the move in France. The Luftwaffe were making heavy attacks on airfields in Kent and Sussex, and the U-boats were on the attack in the Atlantic. On Wednesday 18th September, among the jumble of incoming signals, a W.A.A.F radio operator deciphered the words 'Norman Conquest'. This was from a Luftwaffe unit to an army unit in France. Shortly afterwards a colleague heard the same word used in a message to a naval group in Le Havre. This information was passed on to the intelligence officer who immediately requested any further messages under this code name to be reported at once.

On Thursday 19th September, several more messages were intercepted, all from the same area in northern France. By now the senior officers at Bletchley Park were fairly sure an attack of some sort was being planned, but when? And where? They decided that the code name must have some significance. One of the WAAFs said, "Norman Conquest? Didn't that start at the Battle of Hastings?" It seemed too obvious, and another WAAF said that anyway William the Conqueror landed at Pevensey. However all radio operators were instructed to use their greatest vigilance to find further clues.

On Friday 20th September the pilot of a Spitfire, reporting back after a reconnaissance flight over the French coast, said that he had seen and photographed some transport planes and gliders on the airfield at Abbeville. This news seemed to confirm that airborne troops might be used. Then, at nearly midnight, a short message was intercepted to an airforce squadron at Abbeville. It said only, "Baldslow, 21st September, 5.00hrs. Go." Thinking this was another code word, the WAAF did not react immediately, but the operator sitting next to her saw the message and said, "I know that place, it's a village on the outskirts of Hastings!" Realising that significance they put the signal through to the Duty Officer at once. He immediately summoned the senior staff, and officers who had already gone off duty to be recalled. They decided that there were too many straws in the wind to be ignored, and, at once issued a 'Red Alert' message, "To High Command, South East Area. Possible landing by enemy forces in Hastings area imminent, Prime Minister to be informed."

Throughout the Southeast region sleepy telephone operators got themselves unwillingly out of bed to answer insistently ringing bells. The Baldslow exchange was built on to the side of Bensons the Grocers. When Jack Benson, the owner, closed for the evening he took over the phone duties for the night. As he plugged in the leads to the well-known military numbers, he wondered, "Is this another false alarm, or could it be the real thing?"

The Prime Minister Winston Churchill had left London to spend the night at his country house at Chartwell, near Penshurst in Kent. He never went to bed early, and was relaxing in his easy chair with his cigar and a glass of whisky, when the red scrambler phone rang. His aide answered it.

"It's the CIGS Sir John Dill, Sir" he said. "There are strong indications of a possible enemy landing on the coast at Hastings this morning." Churchill took the phone. Dill said, "We are taking this seriously sir, an armoured column will leave Tunbridge Wells for the coast at first light, do you want to join it?" Churchill thought for a minute. "No, I've got my staff car here, and if the landing is confirmed, I'll get my driver to take me straight there." He did not go to bed, but took up his cigar and whisky and sat reading the latest dispatches, and waiting for the phone to ring again.

Chapter 7

When Hans woke up from his snooze on the garden seat, he enquired about a taxi to take him back to his hotel for lunch. But he obviously wanted to continue looking round, and readily accepted an invitation to have some with us. Over the meal he told us some more about his early life. In the Hitler Youth group they had been told that the Germans were the master race, destined to rule Europe and eventually the World. Hitler had said that the German Reich would last for a thousand years. The German army was superior in manpower and armaments, and would crush all opposition. The easy victories in Poland and France had confirmed this, and had not the British been defeated and forced into evacuation at Dunkirk?

As they had waited for operation 'Norman Conquest' to begin, the talk among the troops had been of an easy ride. A show of force and the British would give up. They had no stomach for the fight! So we were in high spirits as we prepared for our flight. Were we not the troops who had captured the immensely strong forts on the Belgian border? This operation against a little town in Sussex would be a pushover!

I took Hans round the track behind the school to the Cricket Field. He remarked on the changes, and I told him how Hydneye had been knocked down and the new school built, and about the Hospital and the Boundaries building being put up. He gazed across the countryside towards Rye, and from then on he took over the conversation.

"We came in that way," he said, "low over Romney Marsh to keep under the radar screen. Then our towing aircraft climbed to 1500ft to give our gliders height for our run in. We had left Abbeville at 5.00am and we found that the paratroops had already done a good job.

We came to the field and Hans looked round. "They had got the corners marked with flares, and, as there was still a bright moon, the landing area was clearly visible. The dawn light was breaking behind us as we turned to come in. That row of trees across the middle was not there then, and the wooden posts put up to hinder landings had been cut down by the paratroops."

Hans stopped abrubtly and turned to me looking puzzled. "There were some power lines that crossed the corner of the field!"

"Yes," I said, "But they were dismantled thirty years ago."

"I had good cause to remember them." he said, "They gave us our first casualties. The last pilot to come in misjudged his landing and approached too low. The glider caught in the wires and cartwheeled into the lane by the field, exploding in a sheet of flame. The crew of two was killed, but fortunately no troopers as it was our supply glider and carried our heavy equipment.

Nevertheless it was a serious blow as it meant that we should have to go into action without heavy mortars and bazookas."

"Did the rest of you get down all right?" I asked.

"Oh yes, there was no further trouble. Our rendezvous point was the small cottage in the corner of the field by the road. This was empty at the time. We knew the lie of the road, as an agent had been dropped by parachute the previous week and sent back reports."

"I heard about that," I said. "There was a story of a Gypsy woman with a baby in a pram, but she wouldn't let anyone see it, and afterwards people said it wasn't a baby but a radio."

"We weren't concerned with rumour," said Hans, "Our briefing just told us that Hydneye House was occupied by about 50 men of the Royal Sussex Regiment, mostly mechanics, as it was being used as a vehicle repair centre.

They should not prove much of an obstacle as they were lightly armed with no solid defence works."

"So you attacked at once?"

"No, while we re-grouped and checked our weapons, we sent a scouting party to test the Hydneye defences. It also gave time for our young MO Dr Schneider, who had flown with us, to set up his casualty preparations in the Cottage."

"Surely you needed to get on quickly to maintain surprise?" I said.

"We did," said Hans, "Our scouts returned saying that Hydneye was deserted. There were three Bren gun carriers in the yard, but they had no petrol in their tanks. The way seemed clear for us to advance to the bridge. Dawn was breaking as we set off along the road. The time was 6.00am.

Chapter 8

Major Norton had just gone to sleep when the phone rang. "Not another alert," he thought, as he struggled out of bed. "There have been so many lately." He answered the call, and heard Jack Benson's voice.

"Urgent call for you from Southern Command HQ, I think it may be serious this time, putting you through now."

There was no hesitancy in the message from Southern HQ. "Assault by enemy airborne troops expected at dawn, probable objective Harrow Bridge and road junction at Baldslow. Our armoured column preparing to leave. Delay enemy as long as possible.

The major thought for a moment and said to himself, "So it's come at last! And now it's up to us." He called his batman. "Sound the general alarm, and put me through to Hydneye on the field telephone." His second-in-command, Major Bowman came on the line and he quickly explained the situation, adding, "This looks like the real thing. If the enemy land on the Cricket Field you'll be the first to see them. Hold them up as long as you can in whatever way you can. If they are too strong for you, get your men back to the village and join us. We shall be dealing with any landing on the recreation ground."

There was a knock at the door and Sergeant Major Parton entered, "Orders Sir?" he asked.

"Yes, fall in the men in the yard. Detail sections to go to all barricade sites and put the girders in the sockets, and find anything else they can to build them up. Send Corporal Felbridge round the village to tell people to get away if they can, and if not, to get into their air raid shelters. The men are to take full battle kit with them. When they have built up the barricades, they are then to take up positions in the trenches on the bridge approaches and in Harrow Lane."

Major Norton then rang Baldslow Exchange, and Jack Benson answered . "Oh Jack can you get a message through to William Manston's cottage and tell him to get the Home Guard out as soon as he can. They are to go to their positions in the Post Office and Pill Box, and be ready for action at dawn."

He started to put his equipment together, and called his driver to take him up the road to the command post at the Harrow Inn. Then he stopped - one more call, he thought, and rang the Exchange again. "Jack, can you put me through to the Convent please, it's urgent!" He heard the phone ring for some time before it was answered.

"This is the Reverend Mother Milllicent speaking, we only take emergency messages at night."

He replied, hurriedly, "This is Major Norton, local commander Royal Sussex regiment. This is a real emergency, Reverend

Mother. We expect an enemy attack on Baldslow at dawn. Can you tell your Sister Sarah to have all her beds and facilities ready with the utmost speed!"

There was a pause before Reverend Mother's calm voice replied, "You need have no fear, major. We are always ready here."

There was a great rush at Hydneye, with little regard for correct procedure. The alarm had been sounded, and the men appeared from all directions to assemble in the schoolyard.

Major Bowman addressed them, "A substantial force of enemy airborne troops are expected to land at dawn on the Cricket Field. They are expected to attempt to capture the Harrow Bridge and occupy Baldslow. We cannot hold them here, but we can hold them on the road. Get all the vehicles that will move and make a barricade across the road by the upper gate. Then get yourselves dug in on either side of the road. Hold your fire until the order is given, then make every shot count. Are there any questions?"

A corporal said, "Any orders, if the enemy break through, Sir?"

"Yes," he replied, "whistles will be blown to signify disengagement, and you will make your way to Baldslow through the farm fields. When you get there, join the men at the Pub. If there are casualties, they will be taken to St Mary's Convent for First Aid. Take every chance you can to harry the enemy, don't let them rest for a moment. And good luck everybody!" There was a muted cheer as Major Bowman dismissed the men. They began to drive or push the vehicles from the repair shop round the track to the upper gate. By the light of the still bright moon, they built their barricade and dug their trenches. Then they settled down to wait for the attack.

Chapter 9

Hans and I moved out of the Cricket Field on to the road and walked back towards the farm. He re-opened the conversation, "The worst thing was, that we didn't know what to expect. After their defeat in France, and the battering from Goering's Luftwaffe, some of the troops thought the British would give up without a fight. I was not so sure. The British soldier was always a good fighting man, and, on his own soil, defending his own home, he would be twice as good. I didn't like the way Hydneye House was empty, and had a feeling that there was going to be trouble."

"When did you first see the British?" I asked as we crossed the school entrance by the Hospital roundabout and approached the corner. As we came round the bend we could see up the road. "Just about here." said Hans. "Of course the road was narrower then, and the bend sharper. It was just getting light, and we could see the barricade ahead at the top of the slope, but still there was no shooting."

"Did you stop!" I asked.

"No." he said. "The leading troops were ordered to approach the barricade at the double, with weapons at the ready. They were about a hundred yards away, when the British opened fire. It was well directed and steady and two of our men went down. We fired back, but there were few real targets as the British were well hidden in the leafy sides of the road. The bullets clanged and whined as they hit the tram-posts and the stone walls of the Convent grounds. A retreat was called, and we withdrew round the corner to consider the position. We sent some scouts round the back of Hydneye to see if we could outflank the barricade, but they found that there were snipers well dug in the trenches at the back of the farm buildings, and they commanded an approach from that way. We should have to think again."

Sergeant William Manston had installed his Home Guards in the Post Office and the Pillbox. He had seen that they had their instructions and supplies. Was there anything else? "Old Nellie Fisher." he thought, "She won't want to be left out of this." He crossed the road to her house and knocked hard to wake her up. She put her head out of the bedroom window, "What do you want at this time of night?" she said. "The Germans are expected, Nellie, get up to the church as soon as you can. If you hear gunfire you'll know they've come. Then ring the bell, and keep ringing for all your worth!"

Hans and I walked slowly up the road to St Anne's entrance. "This is about where the barricade was," he said. "I knew that we should have to make another attempt to get past, but avoid too many casualties. If we had to fight our way to the bridge, we should need all the troops we'd got."

"Did you charge the barricade again?" I asked.

"Not at once, I knew that we should have some vehicle to push it aside to let us through, but what? Then I thought of the three Bren gun carriers our scouts had said were in the yard at Hydneye with empty tanks. We had brought cans of petrol with us to use in our flame-throwers. Could we get them going? It was worth a try, so I sent a squad back to fetch the petrol and see what they could do. I told them, in any case, to bring the flame-throwers with them when they came."

"You were lucky if you got those carriers going." I said.

"Well they did," said Hans, "and you can imagine my relief when they brought them down the drive. We put five men in each and charged up the slope firing as we went. I was in the leading one and we crashed through the barricade, smashing the vehicles and pushing them aside."

"Were the British firing?" I asked.

"No," said Hans. "Not a shot and when we got through, we found the position abandoned. They had withdrawn to the village. I halted the carriers to let the main force catch up and re-group. It was then that I first heard the bell. That tinny unmusical sound that has haunted me ever since. The troops asked what it was, and I told them that it was the British signal that the invasion had started. Now all the district would know that we were here!"

"That sound was very familiar to us until the road was widened," I said. "It was a shame the church had to close. What was your next move?"

"Well, it wasn't a move, it was a halt. I had called the other officers to consider how we should go on, when we were amazed to see a herd of cows coming down the road. They walked in single file towards us, followed by an old man with a stick."

"That would have been Ben Barrow turning them out after morning milking," I said. Didn't you try to drive them out of the way?"

"No, they seemed to know where they were going, so we just stood and watched. They turned into the convent field here, that I see now is called St Anne's. The old man shut the gate behind them and turned to us and spoke, "I know who you are," he said, "You're Germans. Well you're not stopping my cows getting their grub, and if you take my advice, you'll go back to where you belong. If you go round that corner ahead you'll be in trouble!" and he turned his back on us and walked away.

"We let him go!" Hans continued, "As the carriers had all survived the barricade in working order, we decided to use them in our advance to the bridge. We could hear gunfire ahead, so we knew the other section must have landed at the Recreation Ground and were fighting their way through. There was no time to lose, so we put all the troops we could into the carriers and set off with the others following on foot." The time was 7.00am.

At the farm, the day had started normally. Bert Eldridge, the farmer had helped the cowman with the milking, and sat down to breakfast with his wife, Elsie and their two younger children. The two older children were away. Towards dawn, they heard aircraft, but that was not unusual. At dawn, the gunfire began, and soon after the church bell began to clang. "It must be the invasion," said Bert. "My orders, as a Special Constable are to control the traffic where Westfield Lane joins Ebdens Hill, so I must get off at once." Elsie said, "And I must go over the road to see if Sister Sarah needs help. You two had better come with me."

Hans and I had reached the corner by the Convent gate. We had not hurried because his leg was hurting him.

"I suppose this is where the fight really started hotting up," I said.

His reply took me by surprise. "Well, yes, he said, "but for me this is where the fight ended."

"Did you stop a bullet?" I asked.

"No. Although, when we came round the corner, we did run into heavy rifle fire from the top of the hill. But the armour on the vehicle protected us from that. What did it for me was a grenade thrown over the Churchyard wall. It landed in the back of the carrier and exploded immediately. My leg was shattered and I had wounds in several places from shell splinters. I was in a bad way, but remained conscious and told my troops to put me off and then carry on the attack under my second in command. They gave covering fire while two troopers laid me just inside the Church gateway. As I drifted into unconsciousness the last sound I heard was the clanging of that wretched bell above me.

"How long did you lie there?" I asked. Hans was thoughtful for a minute and then said, "I really don't know, but as I came to, I heard children's voices. A boy and a girl were coming up the path from the farm, carrying a small churn of milk between them. I don't think they can have been older than twelve or thirteen.

The boy said, "He's badly wounded - look at all that blood!"

"Yes," said the girl.

"But he's a German!" the boy exclaimed.

The girl replied, "It doesn't matter what he is, he's a man who's wounded and in pain. "You go to the barn and get the hay trolley, and we'll see if we can get him on that."

"How they did it, I do not know, but they did, and pulled and pushed me over the road and through the gate that had a big Red Cross on it. At the door of the Hospice, we were met by a nurse in nun's habit. I shall never forget her face, and the wonderful look of compassion with which she greeted me. I had met Sister Sarah,"

Chapter 10

The German officers reviewed the situation. A message had come over the field radio from the other assault group, saying that they were being held up by steady and accurate fire from the pillbox and trenches in Harrow Lane. They had lost a number of troopers, and requested immediate assistance. The leading carrier had been put out of action by the grenade, which had injured their CO, but they decided to continue the attack with the other two. They were passing the steps up to the farm cottages on the left, when the British troops hidden in the trenches near the top of the hill, pulled the strings attached to the 45 gallon drums dug into the bank. The bungs jerked out and, as the petrol streamed down the road, a burning rag attached to a stone, was flung into it and the road became a river of flame. The first carrier managed to get through, but the second caught fire and stopped with heavy casualties. The British troops then again withdrew through the gardens to join the men in the village.

Hans and I walked slowly to the top of the hill.

"I suppose you did not know much more about how the battle was going?" I said.

"Oh, but I did," he said, "I was the first casualty to arrive at the Convent First Aid point, but very soon others were brought in. Some had nasty burns from the flaming petrol. They were able to tell me of the action at the top of the hill and what followed."

"Did the remaining carrier continue on towards the village?" I asked.

"Yes," said Hans, "as soon as it was over the hill, it came under fire from rifles in the pillbox, and from the machine gun at the Post

Office. Then the machine gun fire stopped, we think it jammed, so two of our troopers took a flame-thrower and crept down the side of the road where the men in the pillbox couldn't see them. They silenced it with a jet of flame through the firing port that faced up the road."

"Were they able to go through to the bridge after that?" I said.

"No. The girders in the road stopped the carrier, so they left it and went down the road and into the Post Office. The British had abandoned it when the machine gun jammed, so they walked through to the garden and yard at the rear.   There they were joined by the troops from the recreation ground who had got through after the pillbox was dealt with. They were screened from fire from the British by the houses and shops on the corner of Harrow Lane.   Both assault groups had suffered casualties and were dispirited by their failure to break through to the bridge. It seemed a time for a break and refreshment, so the officers told the men to break open some rations while they planned the next move.

Hans was tired, so we sat on the bank opposite the Mill for a few minutes rest. "Tell me a bit more about the First Aid Point." I said.

"Well the First Aid Point was in the old Hospice," he said, "where travellers in olden days could spend the night.   There was only room for six beds, so the Casualty Collecting Centre, the wooden chapel adjacent, had been taken over, and a further eight beds put in. This was again added to later when the Nuns' library was used with beds brought in from the school."

"How did they mange to cope when the casualties were arriving thick and fast?" I said.

"There were several ladies from the village and some of the nuns, and all had had basic training in First-Aid," he said. "I asked to be allowed to speak to the doctor in charge, and told him that our MO Dr Schneider, was looking after the casualties from our first attack, in the cottage along the road. The doctor agreed that they should be brought to the Convent, where our MO could help the medical staff. The place was very busy as you can imagine, but Sister Sarah seemed to be everywhere, organising and encouraging the staff, soothing and sympathizing with the wound- ed. The Convent Chaplain was combining his religious duties with that of stretcher-bearer, being helped by the gardeners.

"You seem to be particularly impressed by Sister Sarah," I said.

"I could not help it," Hans replied. "As one of the most severely wounded, she was constantly by my bed, and under took most of the nursing duties herself."

We got up from the bank and looked down the road towards the village, where the real battle had taken place.

Chapter 11

The time was 7.30am. The Harrow Inn at Baldslow was crowded with British troops. Men of the Royal Sussex Regiment, who had withdrawn from Hydneye, mingled with the Home Guard who had survived the attack on the pillbox and the Post Office. They had found refuge in the beer cellars and behind the sand-bagged walls.

Major Norton and Major Bowman, now together in their command post at the Inn, reviewed the situation. At that moment, there was a standoff, and, although the fighting units were not much more than a 100yards apart, no exchanges of fire were taking place. With no mortars or artillery, neither side could batter down the other's defences. Knowing this, the Germans had called up the Stuka squadron, asking for one well-aimed bomb on the inn to open the way to the bridge. The Stukas had attempted to come inland, but were met over the coast by a squadron of Spitfires. Slow and ill-armed, they turned and fled, except for one that slipped through. A well-aimed burst of fire from a Spitfire, caught it as it turned, and it dived, sirens screaming, into Beauport Park. Word also reached the Inn, that two of the German landing-craft had successfully beached at West Marina and the raiding party of armoured cars and troop-carriers had come ashore almost unopposed. The British officers agreed that there was little that could be done to dislodge the Germans with the forces available. When the armoured column from Tunbridge Wells arrived, further action could be taken. They decided to wait and keep watch.

Bert Eldridge sat in the old, garage buildings at the bottom end of Maplehurst Road. As a special Constable, he had been given the job of directing traffic at the road junction at the approach to the Harrow Bridge. When he heard the Church bell ring, he knew that he must take up his post immediately. Being a farmer, he had been in a reserved occupation in the Great War, and now aged 57 he was too old for military service. Although a first class shot, he had left his 12 bore gun at home, considering himself to be a non-

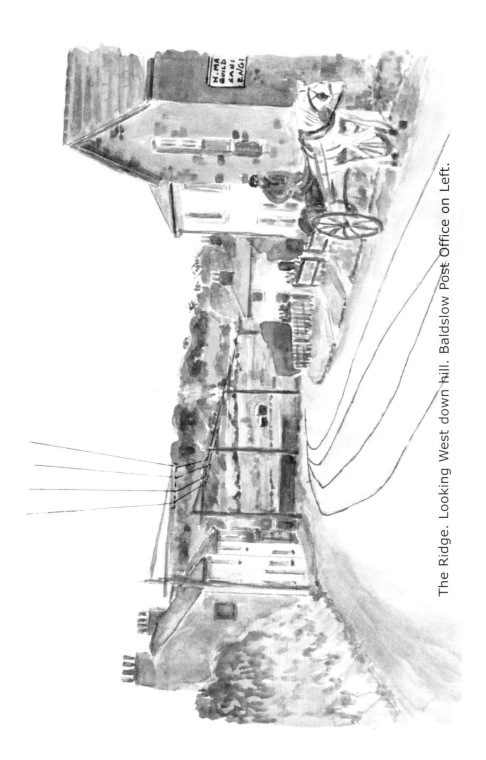

The Ridge. Looking West down hill. Baldslow Post Office on Left.

Baldslow Village. Post Office and Grocers.

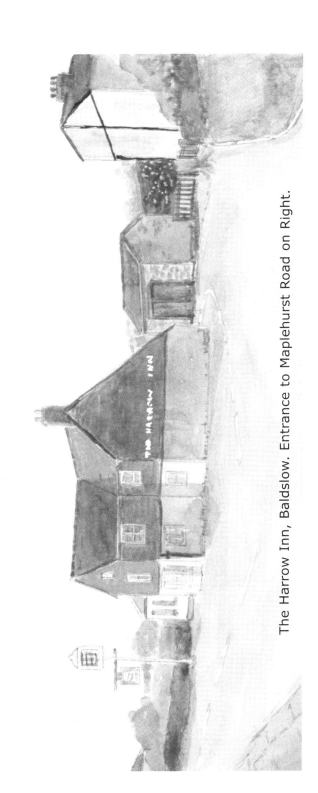

The Harrow Inn, Baldslow. Entrance to Maplehurst Road on Right.

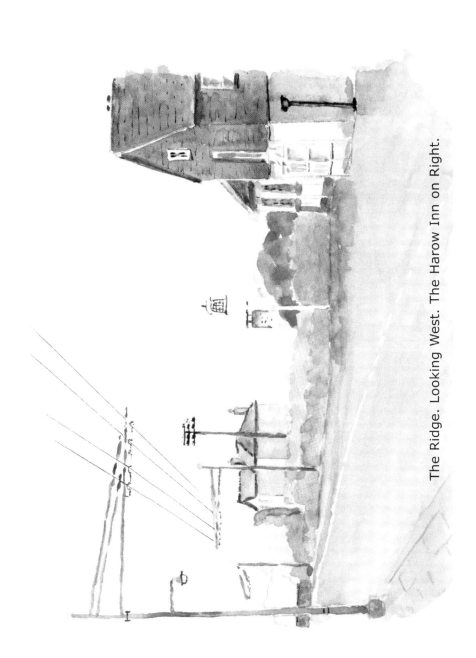

The Ridge. Looking West. The Harow Inn on Right.

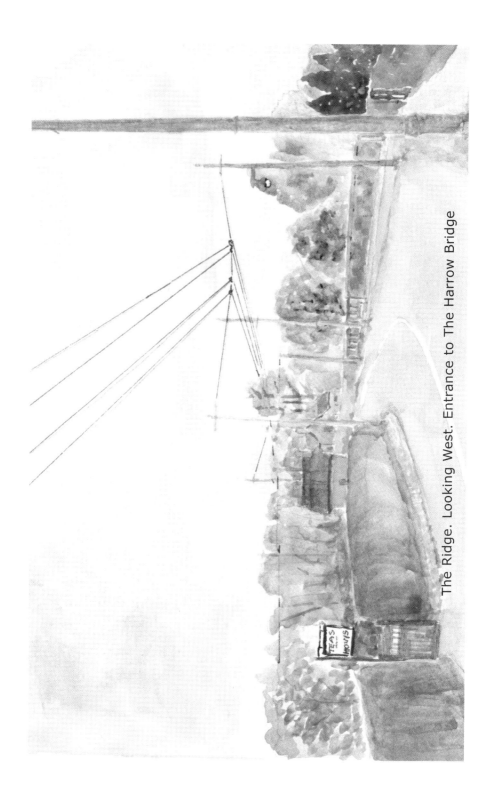

The Ridge. Looking West. Entrance to The Harrow Bridge

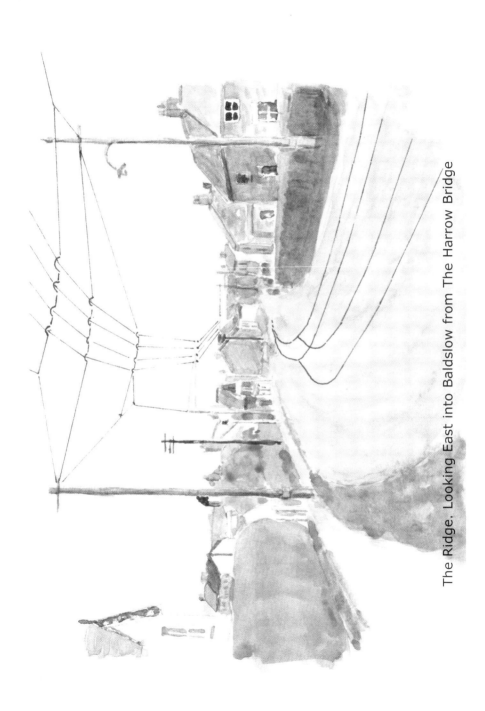

The Ridge, Looking East into Baldslow from The Harrow Bridge

combatant. He was nevertheless glad to be involved in what he felt was going to be vital action. Being a Special Constable now gave him authority for which his local standing made him well fitted.

Occasionally he had had to turn back travellers coming towards Hastings who had not heard the news of the German attack. There had been a moments alarm as the Stuka crashed into Beauport Park nearby. Looking down the hill, he saw a large black Humber car approaching. He stepped out, holding up his hand to signal the driver to stop. Seated in the back was the unmistakable figure of Winston Churchill, dressed as for the House of Commons except for the large service revolver in a holster, strapped to his waist. "Which way to Command HQ?" growled Churchill, not wanting to waste a minute.

"Just up this little hill to the pub," said Bert, "But pull in this lower side or you may be fired on." With no further word, the car sped up the hill.

Major Norton greeted the visitor. "We thought you might come, Sir, but expected you to be with the armoured column."

"Couldn't wait for them," said Churchill, "I always want to be where the action is!" He looked grave, "Do you think the men realise the historic significance of this fight?" he asked.

Some may, but most probably do not," said Norton.

"Call all except the look-outs," said Churchill, "and I will address them." Word had already passed round the pub that Churchill had arrived, and men came crowding in to hear him. Standing on a beer crate, he began, and, with his first words delivered with great oratory and patriotic fervour, he began. "Soldiers, today we fight for England! You fought well in Belgium and in France until let down by our Allies, you fought hard and well for the people of those countries. Today is different. Today, we fight for England, for Sussex, for Hastings. We fight for our homes and our loved ones. We fight to keep our land free from oppression, from the evil tyrant who rules Europe. For 800 years, no invader has triumphed on our shores. We sank the Armada. We overthrew Napoleon, and we will defeat Hitler. It all starts here -today -in this battle. The World is watching. The tide has come so far - today we will turn it and drive the enemy from our land! We fight for England! May God be with us! God save the King!"

A cheer went up and the men talked excitedly while awaiting

orders. Norton turned to Churchill, "Well Sir, you've inspired the men, but what's the next move? We've got to dislodge the enemy from those corner shops before their mobile column gets here and takes the bridge.

Churchill said, "We'll use the oldest trick in the book, remember how the Normans pretended to run away and the Saxons gave chase and were caught in the open?" Norton and Bowman nodded. "Start firing at the doors and windows of the shops, then when they return fire, keep your regulars under cover but let the Home Guard make a show of evacuating the pub where they can just be seen. If they rise to the bait and come out, then the regulars can pick off as many as they can before coming out to engage them on the road. I will lead them!" Norton tried to dissuade him, but he replied, "What do you think I brought my revolver for? I used it at Omdurman, and I will use again today!" And so he did.

Chapter 12

Hans and I walked slowly down the hill to the village. I wanted to talk about the battle, but he seemed to be in a sort of reverie. "All my life, I have thought about those days I spent at the Hospice, and the people I met there. So much blood and hatred met by so much kindness and compassion. Not goody-goody compassion, but hands-on devotion and nursing. Those ladies did not have to do what they were doing. They did it from love of their fellow men under the inspired leadership of Sister Sarah. When they were tired, encouragement from her kept them going. When they were nauseated by blood and injuries, she could bring them back to their duty with a sharp but kindly word."

"Whenever you talk about the Hospice, you mention Sister Sarah," I said, "Why do you think she made such a lasting impression on you?"

Hans thought hard before replying, "I have often asked myself this question. Of course, there was thankfulness. I was a German, an enemy, but it made no difference. She bound up my wounds, and spoke words of kindness and encouragement. But it was not just that, there was something intuitive that was drawing me to her. I felt that this was not all one way. When she did her evening rounds, she seemed to linger by my bed as though there were things she would like to say, but no words were spoken.

We had arrived at the bottom of the hill by the roundabout. "It's all so different now, "I said, "The old shops that sheltered your storm-troopers were pulled down, and new ones built further along to allow for the road improvements."

"Yes," said Hans, "but I saw them before I was sent to P.O.W. camp.

We looked at the short stretch of road between us and the Inn. "Some people agree with Churchill and say this is where the tide turned.

"I think they are right," Hans said. "Until this battle, we had never been beaten. Our great military tradition, and our belief that we were the 'Herrenvolk' - the Chosen Race, meant that we could conquer the World. In a few short minutes, that belief was shattered."

We sat on the box the Council provides for road-grit, and continued our conversation. "So word of the battle reached you quite quickly?" I said.

"Yes," said Hans, "perhaps I'd better tell you all about it." So I settled down to listen.

"It was nearly 9.00am, when our officers decided they must make a move. The deadline for success was 10.00am, after which, if the bridge was not captured, the operation would be called off and our troops evacuated. Word had reached us that the assault group that had landed at Marina was now on its way, and, if the British still held the bridge, they would not get through. Orders were given that the attack was to start at 9.00am, with small groups leaving our base simultaneously, and moving towards the Inn, using any cover they could. We still had our flamethrowers, but to use them effectively, we had to within about 30yards of a target. We planned to get these weapons near the Inn under covering fire and pour jets of fire over the sandbags and into the heart of the building."

"Did your troops see anything of the British?" I asked.

"That's the ironic part of it," said Hans, "Just as our Storm-troops were about to move out, our lookouts called that soldiers were leaving the Inn by the back door and going away down the road behind. Someone shouted, "They're evacuating. Let's go!" and instead of the small groups under cover, our troops rushed down the road together. The British troops caught us in the open, and it was an absolute shambles. After the first volley, the men of the Royal Sussex came out fighting, led by an oldish man in a morning suit. His only military gear was his steel helmet and revolver!"

"That was Winston Churchill," I said.

"So I believe," said Hans, "though our troopers did not know it at the time. They said he was incredible and seemed to have a charmed life. He seemed to be everywhere at once, and encouraging his men, and shouting "God for England, Sussex and St George!" The fight was short and bloody, and we seemed to be getting the upperhand, when a squad of old men, with fixed bayonets on their rifles came charging out of the houses at the top of the road beside the Inn."

"That would have been the Home Guard," I said.

"Well, whatever they were called, they were too much for our troopers. Several of our officers had been killed or injured and the rest had had enough. Weapons were being thrown down and hands put up. Soon those of our troops who were uninjured were being herded into the Inn yard under guard."

"So that was the end of the battle?" I said.

"It was the end of that part of the battle," said Hans, "But it wasn't the end of the fighting." I suggested that we should go into the Inn for a drink, and after that, he could tell me the rest of the story

Chapter 13

The time was 9.30am, and Major Norton re-grouped his men to fight off the German assault group that he knew was approaching from the sea-front. He also knew that the British armoured column from Tunbridge Wells was on its way, and that it was vital to hold the bridge until this arrived. Churchill went with him to inspect the defences. Norton pointed out the girder barricade across the road by the garage, about 100yards from the bridge, and the big tank of petrol on top of the bank with piped leading down to nozzles by the roadside. His men were concealed in trenches on the bank and in the adjacent garden. Churchill sized up the position.

"That barricade may stop the enemy, but we need to destroy him," he said, "Pull it up and make another right in front of the bridge, then they can drive right up to it before they stop, and we can attack them there." Norton's men immediately set about this,
26

and brought all the cars they could from the garage to block the road under the bridge.

Churchill was not satisfied. "Put a man at the road junction behind the bridge, and halt our armoured column there," he said, "then direct part of the force to come up the slip road to the Inn, ready to cross the bridge and go down to the junction road to cut off the enemy's retreat." The light of battle was in his eyes, as he waited with the men, concealed in the trenches beside the bridge. They did not have long to wait, as the German column appeared almost at once, coming up Sedlescombe Road North at a steady pace. It was not as strong as had been intended, as one of the landing craft had run on to the rocks just off-shore, and was unable to land its armoured cars. The column that approached now contained three armoured cars and a personnel carrier with twenty storm troops. The second carrier had broken down with seawater in the engine. It was a force still formidable against the lightly armed men they expected to meet.

I walked with Hans past the grocer's shop, all in one with the building that used to house the telephone exchange in Jack Benson's day. We reached the middle of the bridge, now a con-crete structure with alloy railings, and leant on the parapet look-ing towards the town.

"The road was so much narrower then," he said, "Steep banks on either side made it an ideal place for an ambush."

"How did you get to know about the battle?" I asked.

"Not so much of a battle - more of a massacre," he replied, "One of the crew of the third armoured car was brought into the Hospice with major burns. He told me all about it. There was no sign of the British as they drove up to the makeshift barrier in front of the bridge. Then as they slowed down, the banks gushed petrol and a moment later they were in a sea of flame. He managed to jump out and scramble up the bank, but the other two cars had no chance. The personnel carrier was not affected, but, as they halt-ed, two British armoured cars rushed down the side road and cut off their retreat. Soldiers appeared with weapons trained, and the commander of the British armoured car called out to them to sur-render or be mown down. Wisely they surrendered, and were added to the prisoners already at the Inn.

"Was that really the end of the battle?" I asked.

"Yes," said Hans, "though there were still armed German troops on British soil. The second carrier crew had got their engine going, but, as the deadline for recall had passed, they decided to re-embark in the landing craft. They re-launched and, much to their surprise, managed to make the voyage back unmolested."

"I know why that was," I said, "When Churchill heard that they were re-embarking, he issued an order, saying that they were not to be attacked on the return journey. He wanted them to spread the word when thy got back that the British were ready and waiting for any assault, and would throw an invading army back into the sea. It was a strange situation, because they were shadowed all the way by a British destroyer. The 'Vimy' was on passage from Dover to refit in Portsmouth after the damage she sustained on her gallant trips into Dunkirk. She met the waiting E-boats off Beachy Head, sank two, scattered the rest and then was ordered to see the German landing craft home!"

The day after the battle, Churchill addressed the House of Commons. "All this year," he said, "I have had to tell you of defeats and disasters, damage and destruction, gloom and doom. Today I tell you of a Victory! Yesterday morning a strong Nazi raiding force attacked the Southeast coast at Hastings. They sent their navy - we sank them! They sent their airforce - we shot them down! They sent their invincible storm troopers - they were utterly defeated! This was a small battle, this Second Battle of Hastings, but it was a great victory, because the World now knows that we cannot be overthrown! We shall fight and fight again, and, at the end, we shall be victorious!"

Chapter 14

Hans and I walked slowly from the village. There was no conversation. Perhaps, in silence, he was thinking of his comrades who had died that day so long ago. As we neared the farm, I said, "Well we have covered all the battle field now - is there anywhere else you would like to see?"

His reply, in a way, did not surprise me. "Can we go into the Convent grounds?" He said, "I would like to see the Hospice again." Somehow I knew that, all along, this had been the purpose of his visit.

"The buildings are empty now," I said. "The last of the Sisters moved out three years ago to live in a Monastery in Kent. The property is being sold. The gardeners will have gone home, and

The approach to The Harrow Bridge from South. Junction Road on Left.

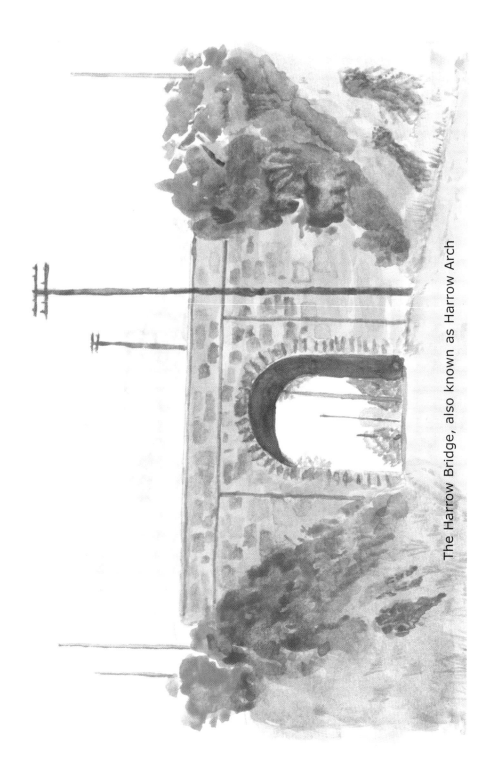

The Harrow Bridge, also known as Harrow Arch

The Hospice at St Mary's Convent.

The Rose Garden at St Mary's Convent

Destroyer and Spitfires off Beachy Head

there is no one to mind if we look round."

We turned in the gate and walked up to the Hospice. Hans was visibly moved, and the emotion showed in his face. Seeing that he was distressed, I moved him on, "Let's go to the rose garden beyond the Chapel," I said. "There are seats there where we can rest." We sat in silence, and the beauty of the surroundings seemed to bring him some peace.

I re-opened the conversation, "When we met first, this morning, you told me that you were on a kind of pilgrimage - a sentimental journey, would you like to tell me about it?"

Hans thought long and hard and said, "It is not a subject that I have ever spoken of, but you have been so kind and sympathetic, that, perhaps I can tell you. Indeed it may do me good to talk about it." He seemed to brace himself, as though he was break-ing through some sort of mental barrier. "When I was severely injured, I was changed, in moment, from a strong, healthy man to a helpless, broken thing, entirely dependent on the ministrations of others. In my weakness and pain, my thoughts were all of thankfulness to those who looked after me and tried to heal my wounds. I lay quite still, marvelling at the skill and devotion of the doctors and nurses who tended me. That first day, I saw many injured men brought in and given first aid. Most were moved on quickly to other hospitals."

"Was that because it was only a casualty collecting centre," I asked.

"That was so," he said. "Only those too seriously injured to move, were kept for any length of time. Sister Sarah was in her element. This was the crowning moment of her life, the moment she had been waiting for. My admiration for her was great, and yet even so, I saw in her, a sense of loneliness. She commanded all around, but was above and beyond them. In all that stress, she had no one in whom she could confide."

"How long did they keep you there?"

"Longer than anyone else," he said, "Some weeks I believe. My dressings were being changed by other nurses, but I saw Sister Sarah every evening when she did her round, and she always stood at the end of my bed longer than at any other - longer than was necessary really. When our eyes met, she would ask gently how I was, and I would reply that I was getting on all right, thank you. That was all, and she would move on to other patients. Not significant, you might think, but I knew, and I am sure she knew, that a bond was forming between us."

It seemed that he was waiting for me to comment, but I could think of nothing to say, so he continued, "An awful thought occurred to me then - I felt that I was falling in love, and more than that, I felt that this feeling was being returned. Can one fall in love with a nun? Ought one to fall in love with a nun? I was a man from an old and honourable family, and I was engaged to a girl at home who was thought to be 'suitable'. Sister was in an Order whose members had professed a vow of chastity. My mind was in a turmoil. One by one the other soldiers left as they got better, the British to sick leave at home, and the Germans under escort to prison camps. At length, I was the only one left."

I felt it was now time to comment. "That must have been a very difficult situation for you," I said.

"Yes," said Hans, "with every patient that left, Sister Sarah seemed to shrink a little. Her little empire was crumbling and soon she would have to return to the confines of her Order. Already the dispensations granted her to run the Hospice were being withdrawn. I had given my parole not to escape, and was allowed to walk in the grounds by day. One morning, we met in this rose garden. No words were exchanged, but her look of desperation and longing was agony for me. Soon after, I heard that orders had come for my transfer to a prison hospital. On the day that I was to leave, I knew that I should see her when I was discharged. I picked a beautiful red rose in this garden, and gave it to her as she raised her eyes from the discharge book. She could not look at me, but got up swiftly and left the room, taking the rose with her. I never saw her again. All these years I have longed to meet her once more, and that is why I came back.

"Why has it taken so long for you to return?" I asked

"I have often asked myself that," said Hans, "but I had five years in a POW camp. Then repatriation and marriage to the 'suitable' girl, which proved quite happy and produced four children. Then, last year, my wife died, and with the children grown up, I was free to follow up this passion of long ago. Can you help me find her?"

"Yes, "I said gently, "Come with me." He gathered some roses as we went.

We walked down a leafy track to a clearing on a sunny bank. Here the War Graves Commission kept the turf and gravestones of a small cemetery in immaculate order, with Germans on one side and the British on the other. Hans stopped occasionally in front of an inscription to bow his head in salute. We moved on beyond to the Convent cemetery, even smaller, with rows of stark little iron crosses only inscribed with the simple Christian name of a Sister and the date of her death. Hans knew then why I had brought him there, indeed, I think he must have guessed it already. I led him to a grave quite near that of the Reverend Mother.

"She lies here," I said. "You see, she did not last long after the war. I came to her funeral. One of the Sisters told me that, after she died, some rose petals were found pressed in her prayer book. They said she had died of heart failure."

Hans knelt by the grave and placed his roses near the cross. He looked up at me and there were tears in his eyes, "They were wrong," he said, "She died of a broken heart."

Spiritual guides
in the West Country

Jane E White

Bossiney Books · Launceston

to all our guides — thank you

Author's acknowledgements
I am grateful to all who have contributed to this book in any way, and
would particularly like to thank Patrick Gamble for permission to
reproduce his painting on the front cover. The photographs and drawings
inside the book have been kindly supplied by the people interviewed,
except those on pages 37 and 50 which are from my husband's collection.

First published 2001 by Bossiney Books
Langore, Launceston, Cornwall PL15 8LD

Printed and bound by R Booth (Troutbeck Press), Mabe, Cornwall

Introduction

Since moving to the West Country a few years ago under rather fraught circumstances, I've discovered that my new home is not, as I first believed, a bleak place tucked away at the bottom of the world. There are buzzards on my doorstep which sail and spiral overhead on warm summer air currents. A short drive away there are sandy beaches and rocky coves echoing to the crash of waves, and windswept cliff tops embroidered in the spring with golden yellow, pink and mauve. And for rich contrast in the autumn and winter months bronze-coloured moorland, often dusted with snow on the highest peaks, is streaked with streams glistening like mirrors in the sun.

I haven't always been so mellow. Before uprooting to Cornwall (a distant place, I had thought, where people only went for holidays) I clung to the trappings of success in London. The ultimate dilemma for any 'career woman' eventually came when I'd allowed my strength and health to be beaten out of me: should I or shouldn't I resign from my job? But even as each day brought more and more difficulties, I kept pushing a decision to one side. Finally, one morning as I was being hurtled from A to B on the tube, I witnessed a bizarre scene.

Opposite me a young boy, with tousled blond hair and long-socked legs dangling over the seat, sat next to his mother. On his lap lay a large English dictionary and the word the two of them began discussing as I looked on was, curiously enough, 'resignation'. Pure coincidence? During this period of deliberation I also found little collections of coins – two or three at a time – nearly every day on the ground in the car park. Did these signify 'change' of circumstances? In hindsight it was as though someone or something was trying to give me a message: be bold and accept the risk of moving.

Reluctantly, I quit my job and career, and left the comfort of my cosy middle England niche. Now, having adjusted to a different way of living and content with the glorious countryside

3

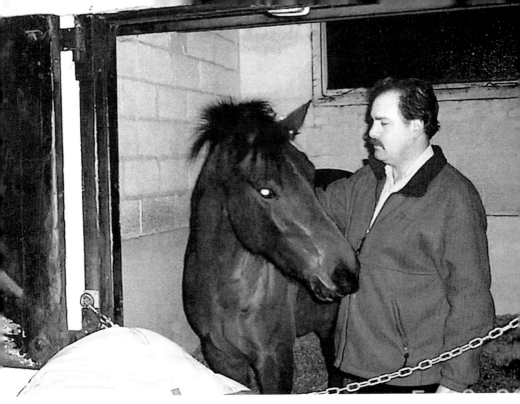

Martin Cox, horse whisperer and animal healer, whom I met 'by chance' in an ambulance!

all around me, I often contemplate the power behind the awesome beauty here and what brought me, seemingly against my will, to a place of recuperation and growth. Was I indeed guided? And if so, why and by whom?

I've bumped into other people with equally strange experiences to relate who are also searching for answers to similar questions and who, like me, are drawing comfort from living in the south west. Each is what I would call a 'spiritual' person. Not necessarily tied to any one religion, they are actively seeking in their own individual ways to become more loving human beings by weaving into their everyday lives the strands of truth that are common to all religions.

Some have lived in the West Country since the day they were born, while others talk openly of having been brought much further distances than the one I journeyed. Most believe they are following some sort of divine guidance and that everyone is helped, knowingly or unknowingly, by beings or energies outside our physical realm. All are now in turn offering practical help, encouragement and, where appropriate, spiritual guidance to fellow travellers wobbling along the world's rickety paths.

The idea for a book to record on paper a few of their fascinating insights into life's deepest mysteries came to mind about a year ago when I was just becoming aware of my own spiritual quest. I was then faced with the quandary of who to ask – I wished to reflect a wide variety of interests, talents and spiritual gifts (clairvoyance, healing, channelled drawing and so on), but in those early days didn't know many people.

I needn't have been concerned, as the choice of who to approach seemed to be decided for me, and in some cases our way of meeting was quite extraordinary. I met Martin Cox, for instance, in a private ambulance (a long story for another book!) while taking a relative to a nursing home. Under normal circumstances he wouldn't have been on duty, but that day he'd agreed to fill in for someone else at short notice.

The drive took just ten minutes, but during that brief chunk of time he unintentionally mentioned his healing work with animals. I was particularly taken aback because, not only was I looking for people to interview, but one of my cats was seriously ill and an animal healer was just what I'd been hoping to find. It was synchronicity at its best...

Twelve months on, my writing task is now complete, and all that remains for me to do is to thank each person who appears in this book for so generously giving of their time and for sharing their fabulous stories. I have learned an enormous amount from every one of them, and I hope their words and deeds prove as thought-provoking and inspirational to readers as they did to me.

Thomas, a medium

There is a beautiful winding road that sweeps down to Bideford through woods and lush green fields. Suddenly you're crossing an inlet, looking to see what the tide has left in the earth-brown mud and almost tasting the salt in the brisk sea air.

Bideford is where Thomas, as he likes to be known, has lived for around 25 years. He is a warm, gentle man in his sixties with a honed sense of fun and humour, often at his own expense. When we first met I thought how unlike a medium he was, but then what should a medium be like – middle-aged, female, lots of beads and gold earrings, long black hair held together with combs, brightly polished finger nails encircling a crystal ball?

Apart from not looking his age, Thomas is just like you or me, with household chores to keep up with and weekly shopping runs to be made. But there is a bewitching twinkle in his eye which hints at something else in his life, something obviously very special to him.

He was born at the foot of Kit Hill in Cornwall. His mother loved reading tea leaves and cards, but it wasn't until he was much older and bought a few books by Edgar Cayce (a well-known American visionary in the early 20th century) that he began to think more seriously about other worlds and realities.

He trained as a ladies' hairdresser and, after some time in New York, he returned to the West Country, to Bideford, where punk fashion hit the streets within a matter of weeks. Those coloured spiky gel quiffs just weren't to his taste or style at all, so he felt compelled to change career and his compassionate nature led him towards nursing.

Thomas qualified as a male auxiliary nurse and found the job wonderfully rewarding. Then he was suddenly catapulted into looking at life from a very different perspective. As he now comments, with a playful look on his face, 'That's when "it" happened… Personally I feel that some of us have to have a traumatic event happen to us, which knocks us sideways, to get

us onto the spiritual path.'

What 'it' meant was that, after the devastating break-up of his marriage, Thomas joined the local spiritualist church in Bideford and began his real adventure into the unknown. With a little prompting from friends both here and beyond, Thomas was able to nurture his own gifts through the church's 'development circle'. Under the guidance of an experienced medium who, amongst many things, taught him how to meditate, and with much hard work on his part, he gradually gained a better understanding of what (or perhaps that should be 'those whom'), with fingers pointing upwards, he calls 'them up there'.

Thomas wasn't always a willing student, and at times he stubbornly refused to play ball.

'At the beginning of my development,' he says, 'I had a very strong argument with various people up there. I told them that I was quite willing to do whatever they wanted, but I was not willing to be taken over completely. At the end of the day if I don't want to listen, I won't!' He laughs, and then continues, 'We all talk to ourselves, but I know that when I'm talking, someone else is listening and will answer back in unexpected ways – often using different words and phrases from mine.

'One day I was lying in the bath. I'd been going through a difficult patch and a friend said I needed to relax. She'd recommended some aromatherapy bath oil, so there I was, with bubbles floating round me. Out of nowhere I heard an Irish voice talking to me. It was a very broad accent, and the language was strong and to the point! I was a bit taken aback, thinking "This is really weird. This has never happened in the bath before!"

'It turned out he was an Irish tinker who'd died in 1800 from what he described as "the cold". At first I didn't understand what he meant, but my nursing training clicked in and I asked him whether he'd died of hypothermia. He said, "I don't know, but I was found on the moors and because of what people did to me I died." I soon realised he meant his rescuers didn't bring his temperature up gradually, as you should when someone's suffering from extreme cold, and that had been his downfall.

'He's been with me ever since. Once, I'd taken a trip up to Scotland to visit my brother for a couple of days. We had a very pleasant time and I drove back, minding my own business. Then, as I got to the new bridge at Bideford, a little voice said with a sigh, "To be sure 'tis good to be home now!" I asked, "Who are you?" and he said, "You know who I am. I've been with you all the time, but I've kept quiet!"

'These days I can usually tell when he's around, because I get this bubbly, cheerful feeling. I think he's there to make me feel better. He helps me when I'm giving messages, and sometimes I'll come out with his broad Irish accent – though his language has toned down a lot!'

Not only does Thomas hear voices, but he also has clairvoyant abilities. In other words he sees images. He points to the middle of his brow, and indicates that he receives pictures there, through his 'third eye'. Only the other weekend he was giving a message to a young man when all he could see were a pair of feet and lower legs, wrapped in the sort of puttees worn by soldiers in the 1914–18 war. Usually an image builds up for him into a full portrait, but this time it stopped at knee height.

The young man asked Thomas a very pertinent question, and then the figure materialised completely. At the time Thomas felt the spirit had been waiting for this particular enquiry before making himself known fully – and so both he and the message had a much greater impact as a result.

Providing such significant, very personal images or information known only to the recipient is not, apparently, uncommon. Not long ago a lady was amazed when Thomas said he knew there was someone in the church congregation who was always checking that the gas had been turned off in her house. She admitted she was constantly doing this, so she felt the subsequent message would be especially relevant for her. No one else in the room had any problem over gas safety at all!

Sometimes Thomas experiences physical sensations, too. If, for instance, some one in the spirit world had a leg amputated when they were alive, Thomas will have no feeling in his own leg. Or he might be touched on the arm or face by an unseen presence. 'All sorts can happen,' he muses, 'and in meditation you look forward to it because there's always such a nice feeling.

'I think the main thing when you're working is to be truthful. If something comes through and I'm not a hundred per cent sure of it, I'll say this is the impression or feeling I'm getting. I don't place an importance on who's giving me a message and they don't always impress on me who they are. The first time I ever stood up in front of people, I was petrified, and in the early days I also found it difficult to accommodate people's disbelieving attitudes, because you do get an inkling of whether someone is trying to block you or is not really accepting. Now, though, I realise I'm not responsible for the messages I'm giving. My job is to be a channel. And if I give only a few or even just one message in one evening I've still done my job.

'I'm not in the business of fortune telling, either. I was recently asked to go on a morning television programme about young women and their spiritual advisers. I declined, because

I'm not here to tell people how to live their lives, but to help them come to terms with what happens in their lives. It seems that some folk won't do anything without first consulting a guru of sorts – be it a psychic or an astrologer. It wouldn't be right to have that amount of control.

'And, after all, any one can do what I do. You just have to put faith and trust in yourself and in your God, however you may perceive him/her. I usually suggest to people that they go with their gut reaction. If you're in a bookshop, see what you're drawn to or whether a book jumps out at you. Read it and listen to someone else's point of view. You don't have to take it on, but it might open up your mind a bit further.'

In the early development circle days, a group member astonished Thomas by telling him that he had had a past life in Peru. He was supposed to have undertaken much spiritual work then but, even though he had helped many people, he became too much of a recluse and didn't achieve everything he had set out to do. The concept of reincarnation didn't faze Thomas at all and he did not discount the information; in fact he found the comments rather helpful – at least he knew what he was supposed to do this time around!

Since then he has come to realise he has a spirit 'doorkeeper', Jeremiah, a sort of guardian who protects him, prevents him picking up negative vibrations and helps him interpret messages. He believes that Jeremiah, now his constant companion, is someone he has known before and had a strong bond with, and that while he came to the physical world, Jeremiah stayed in the spirit world. 'I don't disbelieve in angels,' Thomas smiles, 'but I'm a very down to earth man and need another person – not someone with wings – who I know has been on the earthly plane before and has gone through the sort of things we all have to experience. When I stand up at the rostrum in church I know Jeremiah is there and that's comforting – I have to be very strong in my faith when I look out at the sea of faces!

'From what I can gather everyone has their own doorkeeper,

and it doesn't matter whether you're aware of them or not. They are there from the minute we're born until we pass over.'

In some instances Thomas receives messages from a person's own doorkeeper. On one occasion he was talking to a young woman when he noticed someone materialising behind her who communicated with him telepathically. After he had given the woman all the information he could, she told Thomas, 'This is the first time I've had a message like this. Everything you said, including things you weren't aware of, was all true!'

He even manages to strike a chord with groups of people during his general church addresses (rather like 'sermons', but Thomas dislikes the word as it smacks of preaching). It is not uncommon for individuals to approach him afterwards and say warmly, 'Your talk really meant something to me. Where did it come from?' to which Thomas has to admit, 'I just open my mouth and it comes through…'

Such complimentary remarks may not be the norm in the future, for he is now approaching a period in his life when he feels compelled more and more to comment on others' spiritual development. At first he was reluctant to pursue this particular route, but strong direction from 'them up there' has made the path clear. 'If I suggest to someone they're putting too much emphasis on material goods,' he says, 'they're not necessarily going to like it. But if that's what I sense, that's what I'll tell them! It's then up to them whether they accept it…'

Will Thomas ever leave the West Country? His work often takes him up to Bridgwater and down to Wadebridge, and anywhere in between, and he's been told he may go further afield in the future. But he cannot bear to live far from the sea and believes that the south west is like a strong magnet which is drawing spiritually minded people to it. He read somewhere that the most popular car sticker in New Orleans is 'He who dies with the most toys, wins'. That's a far cry from his own life in which for him quality of being far outweighs the transient thrills of the rat race.

Martin Cox, animal healer, and Sue Cox, past life researcher

A crush on a visiting French teacher at school was an unlikely starting point for Torquay animal healer Martin Cox who can also scan people's bodies like an X-ray. 'We were on a weekend trek,' he recalls, 'and the French teacher had a bad migraine. I was helping organise the trip, so I felt responsible for everyone. I also had other things on my mind!

'Eventually I plucked up courage and told my teacher I would help get rid of her headache by tracing my fingers about her head. I asked her to imagine the tips were a downhill skier.

'She later said she felt cold, and then experienced a warm feeling as though I was wrapping myself round her. Her migraine disappeared totally. As a sixteen year old, I thought I was a rather naughty schoolboy wanting to be near someone I was fond of, but years afterwards I realised I was actually healing her.'

Martin is a tall, robust man in his early forties who radiates energy and caring. He grew up in a sports-mad environment, and became more than competent at a wide range of activities (but hates football with a vengeance). Quite early on he trained an athlete who went on to represent Great Britain at the Los Angeles Olympics, though he has to admit the person lost in the first bout…

Curiously, he is often around whenever there is an accident and he invariably knows instinctively what to do. Before he moved to Torquay, his ability to calm people just by talking to them came into its own when he qualified as a paramedic/ambulanceman and coping with accidents became all part of a day's work! The skill extends to animals, too. One day a man was brought into the casualty department of Torbay Hospital, where Martin is now a porter, after having been hit by a car. Outside, the man's dog, which had also been involved in the accident but wasn't physically hurt, was in a frenzy. The dog warden had been summoned; Martin, however, decided the quickest and best course of action was for him to enter the fray instead.

By now the creature was extremely agitated, barking furiously, frothing at the mouth and eyes glazing over. Martin got on his hands and knees so that his eyes were on the same level as the dog's, much to the consternation of staff and visitors gathering round, and he then placed a bowl of water in front of it. He literally asked it what all the fuss was about and told it there was nothing to worry about. Still agitated, but no longer barking, the dog came and sat next to him, put its head on his shoulder, and sighed. After he suggested it should have a drink, it lapped the water, lay down and allowed Martin to stroke it. He then took it inside the hospital where the owner was being treated, after which the animal was content, safe in the knowledge that all would be well.

Martin would never advise anyone else to put themselves at risk in this way. His complete confidence stems from an inner knowing, an innate understanding of animal behaviour which he cannot explain but which tells him how to react to any situation he chances upon. It has helped him especially with horses, such sensitive creatures that they can detect fear in a human and can be aggressive to the point of being dangerous. For Martin, though, the bigger the horse, the easier it is. 'Smaller ponies fight amongst themselves to see who's boss,' he muses, 'but a $17^{1}/_{2}$ hands hunter is a dream. I might expect to be kicked or bitten, but all that's happened to me has been a quick nibble.'

He was once called to the aid of a woman whose experience was very different: every time she put a blanket on it, she was bitten by her horse. She just couldn't break the vicious cycle. As usual, a crowd were standing round, waiting to see what Martin would do. He first asked the woman to show him exactly how she performed the task and as soon as she went under its belly, it swung its neck round, eyes glaring defiance, and sank its fiercesome teeth into her raised behind. She immediately remonstrated, naturally exasperated and probably humiliated too by the horse's cussedness.

Martin takes up the story. 'I then had a go. I showed him the blanket and told him I knew nothing about this, but it had to go on him for his own benefit. I explained where I would be touching him and clipping the blanket, and finished off by saying, "I don't want your teeth on me. OK?"

'By now everyone was sniggering, including the horse, but I carried on. I stroked him, placed the blanket in position, stroked him again, clipped it under his chest, bent down under his belly presenting my rear end as a huge temptation, lifted his tail right up and fastened the last clip. I then put my hands over his head, stroked him and said goodbye. It was sheer guesswork, but I knew the horse was working with me.'

From then on the horse never bit his owner again.

It would seem that healing works in many ways and on different levels, not just the physical. And perhaps this is why Martin has, until comparatively recently, felt stigmatised. He admits that for a long time he was embarrassed to talk about or even use his gifts openly, because of the reactions from other people who intimated, to use Martin's own characteristically humorous phrases: 'You're off your trolley', 'You're on another planet', 'The lights are on, but there's no one there.' It was as though he had some intolerable disability but, with encouragement from his twin brother who had already completed a healing course, he joined the Teignmouth branch of the National Federation of Spiritual Healers.

With other members' help, he came to understand that for him healing is perfectly natural and not to be hidden away. 'Today,' he states, 'people are beginning to come round. Even my GP is open to it.' Not all doctors have the same view, but Martin has certainly helped broaden the mind of at least one in Torbay Hospital.

Several years ago, Sue (Martin's wife and a nurse at the hospital) was talking to this particular doctor in an office. They were discussing Martin's healing abilities and Sue also mentioned how he could scan someone's body. Just at that moment, Martin came into the room and was immediately put on the spot by the doctor who demanded to know what was wrong with him.

Pausing briefly, Martin quickly scanned him, and then informed him he had a pain in the back of his right knee, about a centimetre deep under the skin. The doctor's reaction was one of indignation. 'How did I get it?' he again challenged, to which Martin retorted, 'That's unfair! I've told you what you wanted to know!' And with that he turned away and, trying not to smirk, walked out.

The doctor left the hospital shortly after this episode for duties elsewhere, but returned three years later. He sought Martin out and in time even referred patients to him. His view about healing is now markedly different, and he will chat about ghosts and spiritual matters with great enthusiasm.

But how did Martin *do* it, how did he know where the pain was in the man's leg? He explains the scanning phenomenon in terms of a line he sees which moves down the body and flashes up 'hot spots' where there is an injury or an illness. He has even performed this feat on someone thousands of miles away.

Quite recently he was speaking on the phone to a relative in New York and, as they were chatting, Martin imagined his cousin leaning to the left-hand side. He deduced that a pain was shooting up from the man's left ankle and pushing his hip out. His cousin was 'totally amazed' when Martin commented on this, because nothing had been mentioned about the troublesome niggle during their conversation. Not only that: Martin directed his cousin's daughter, whose own healing abilities are just beginning to develop, to the precise hot spots needing treatment and within a few minutes the pain had gone.

Martin's local pharmacist will also vouch for his extraordinary accuracy. He was able to detect in her otherwise healthy body just one scar, perhaps from an appendicitis operation but very small. She was stunned: five years previously she had undergone a laparoscopy, a minor investigative operation which had left her with a little scar in the place Martin had indicated.

Since then she has become a staunch supporter of his work and will spend much time and effort researching suitable aromatherapy oils and alternative medicines for his patients. Martin believes firmly in the efficacy of a wide range of therapies to complement his 'hands on' healing, and will select whichever he feels is most suitable. Laminitis in hoofed animals, for example, can be very painful and difficult to treat. But with a specially mixed herb poultice, one lucky horse was cured in no time at all.

Another horse, which had eaten ragwort several months earlier and had liver failure as a consequence, was not so fortunate. Martin was brought in very late in the day, by which point a successful physical recovery was always going to be in doubt. The ideal situation for him is to be introduced to the conventional treatment team early on, which often means working alongside vets and not being used as a last resort. But he understands why he is often contacted by people who have reached desperation point.

With animal patients (whom he secretly prefers, but only because of his lifelong bond with animals) he likes to be near them: experience has shown that they respond favourably to his touch, and he can feel and control where the healing is going. To start with he will sense the creature's energy around it, its aura. Next he will 'balance' this by following his own specially devised routine, working from side to side and from the head downwards. Only then will he home in on the spots needing healing. For human patients he has a similar system, but in deference to their modesty touch is confined to the back and legs. There is often a sensation of heat, though sometimes this can be of cold.

Martin himself feels a deep sense of calm, as if 'my aura is

A wild fox successfully treated by distant healing

twice as big as usual and is enveloping the person or animal I'm working with. When I first started healing, though, I used to be drained by the whole experience and I would become exhausted. Now I've learned how to protect myself and this no longer happens.'

But what if Martin can't get to a patient? Can he still help? The answer would seem to be yes, through 'absent or distant healing'. A friend of his, living at Newton Abbot, had managed to form such a close relationship with a wild fox that it would often come into her house. She became concerned, however, when she noticed the creature was developing mange, a usually fatal disease. She got in touch with Martin and he asked for a photograph. This she gladly provided, showing the fox in her living room, front paws on the sofa, stealing crisps out of her hand!

Martin then began the process of absent healing. I ask him how he goes about this and he gives me a brief explanation: 'The photograph goes up on the mirror in the hallway. For a couple of days I just glance at it. After about a week I eventually get through to the animal – I know where it is and can picture it in its surroundings. Once the scene is set up, I can then communicate with it. It's not verbal, it's just something my mind tells me and I can pick up where the illness or disorder is. I narrow it down and concentrate on the injured part. For example, if there's a digestive problem, I'll imagine squeezing the intestines all the way down until the badness comes out at the end. I'll spend ten to fifteen minutes doing that, then ten to fifteen minutes building up the aura. Once I've got good protection round the animal, I'll back off, leave it and go back in a couple of days.

'It's the animal that does the healing: all I'm doing is triggering it. I also encourage it to think positive. Cats will often bring "presents" to their owners – one of ours once brought us a live adder onto the bed. It just lay there! Instinct told me it wouldn't bite me, so I picked it up and took it outside. But I do get really spooked by big spiders!'

Needless to say, the fox recovered and six months later proudly turned up at the lady's house in Newton Abbot with her cubs.

All wild creatures have a particular fascination for Martin, and this has led to some amazing incidents at Paignton Zoo. He thought it would be interesting to see if he could communicate with one of the animals there. He and Sue happened to be by the tigers' enclosure and the magnificent beasts were pacing up and down waiting to be fed. When food is in the offing, most zoo animals, tigers especially, will not be distracted by anyone or anything: they are concentrating solely on that trap door opening and food appearing.

Children were banging with frustration on the glass, but were ignored by the tigers. Martin then tried to reach the big cats through his mind. After about a minute, one of them stopped three metres from him, turned his head and looked straight at him. Sue remarked how it was as though the tiger had suddenly come up against a brick wall and how the unusual behaviour was stunning to observe.

Martin knew he had got through to the animal, which subsequently walked off but kept coming back to look at him. He and Sue were even more astounded when another tiger came right up to the glass, within millimetres of Martin, to see who he was. 'The hairs all over my body stood right up!', recalls Martin, 'I never realised before how good it could get…'

On a separate occasion he put his hand up against the glass wall surrounding a monkey pen. One of the monkeys came from way over the other side and placed its hand on the glass inside, matching Martin's position exactly. 'This really freaked us out!' he says, 'And it set me thinking about the next stage in my development – to work with wild animals.'

Coincidentally, a short while later he was taking a patient to the fracture clinic when during their conversation he learned that the man he was wheeling down the corridor was none other than a keeper at Paignton Zoo. He told the keeper about his love of animals, the experiences he'd had at the zoo and his healing gifts, and the keeper immediately invited him to visit. 'Zoos like healers,' he'd apparently commented, 'because vets don't like getting in there with all those teeth and claws!'

As Paignton did not have a local healer to call on, Martin was delighted at the news. No pay, but a chance to fulfil a dream when the time is right for him.

Martin's wife Sue is also devoting her resources to helping others. She has lived in the West Country all her life and has been a nurse for 17 years or so.

Her very early introduction to what could loosely be termed paranormal events came about after her father suddenly collapsed and died at her feet when she was only two years old. She was brought up in her grandmother's house where for a long time she shut out the trauma of her father's death, but she and the rest of the family could not ignore a presence that would switch lights on and off and move objects around. They eventually discovered the house had been built on a press-gang route and that the spirit – who had come to protect Sue – was that of a woman who had lived during the Napoleonic era.

Growing up with odd happenings taking place all around her, Sue soon came to the conclusion 'there is something else rather than just the here and now'. It is only within the last couple of years, however, that she has felt drawn to working with some of the energies she senses.

'I can walk into a place and tell if "someone" is there,' she admits, 'and sometimes, if I don't like the feel of somewhere I'll ask Martin to get me out, quick! Occasionally I'll catch a glimpse of spirits, but I mainly feel their presence – although recently we were playing darts in a local pub and someone was telling me in my ear not to throw in a certain way. When that sort of thing happens it can be quite unnerving. Berry Pomeroy Castle really scares me. There is a point on the road from Marldon down to the castle where presences literally seem to wham into me. But Martin has taught me how to protect myself, so these things don't get to me as much as they used to.'

She explains that her psychic abilities were moved on substantially when Martin's twin brother Steve, a psychic artist, showed her a picture of a woman who had asked him for a drawing. Steve really wanted Martin's help with healing for this lady, but he happened to give Sue the photograph. It showed an unremarkable scene of a woman standing in front of a gate.

As Sue was staring at the image, something extraordinary happened. The background in the photograph disappeared and all she could see was the same woman hanging from a gallows. Sue was shocked rigid and yet she 'knew' why this person had been hanged, that her name was Mary, how old she was, where the execution had taken place, the fact that she had a daughter she was distraught at leaving, and so on. While Sue rattled off all this information, Steve's and Martin's chins dropped further and further towards the floor. They were awestruck by the whole event.

Sue never met the woman in the picture, but what Sue had discovered about her past life was conveyed to her. At first the woman was badly shaken by the news, and then later she revealed why: curiously she had always hated any clothing or jewellery round her neck and she had an almost obsessional relationship with her daughter who she constantly worried would be taken from her in some way. With this new knowledge about herself, she is now learning to move on and leave behind her old fears.

Sue believes that each reincarnation is all about learning. The twist in the tale is that we don't usually know what the lessons are unless someone like her is able to give us a few pointers. She and Martin agree many people have difficulty with the idea of reincarnation, but Martin has a bizarre personal experience to relate which might provide some food for thought.

'I'd tried regressing to a past life once before, with a professional hypnotherapist, but nothing had happened. I decided to give it another go. This time what felt like a few seconds went by and I told the man to start the tape recorder. He said, "Start? It's been going for the last half hour. Don't you remember?" I didn't – I had no idea I had said anything until they played the tape back to me. As far as I was concerned I'd only been on the couch a couple of minutes at most.

'On the tape I described myself as a Spitfire pilot during the Second World War. I was escorting Lancaster bombers across the Channel, and I and one of the Lancasters were shot down. We were all rescued, and I recalled being hooked up in some way at my back to a boat. I knew I wasn't one of the Lancaster crew because I was dressed differently.

'We later did some research and actually traced this person whose name I knew from the regression (though I'd prefer not to mention it out of respect for his family). He was an RAF Spitfire pilot in Number 1 Squadron, stationed at Shoreham in

Sussex, who was on escort duties towards the end of the war. There is a clear record of this pilot from a hop-growing family in Kent having been shot down together with a Lancaster bomber... I get goose pimples just talking about it.

'It's possible I could have read about the scenario, but I'm not a book-reader so it's highly unlikely. And I don't see how I would have known the names of the man's brothers or of his father. The only way of finding out all of this was through my brother whose hobby is flying planes and who later got access to the museum at Shoreham.'

Strangely enough, Martin can no longer remember much of what he spoke into the tape that day. Most of it has gone from his mind.

Since the photograph episode, Sue has continued to do similar 'psychometric' readings for other people. She knows she is being assisted by her own special guides. I ask her whether she is consciously aware of them and her answer is yes: 'If I'm at home doing the dishes, I might see something fleetingly in my peripheral vision. Or I might sense someone standing behind me. And when I'm doing my readings, I can often feel the weight of a hand on my shoulder.' Martin here confesses he once saw a figure standing at the back of Sue, although he wasn't aware at the time that she was in the middle of a reading.

Sue believes one of her guides, Tek (a shortened version of a rather lengthy name), was a native American who, like her, is still learning spiritually, but who is in another dimension. Her obvious affinity with native American culture for many years is evident from the artefacts fondly displayed around their house. According to Sue, Tek was influential in steering her towards using shamanistic type 'medicine cards' for her readings.

As many of these are done without the person concerned being present, she puts together a document for them. When she starts writing, she can't stop – she has to keep going until every last word has been written, even if this means staying up until the small hours of the morning. Sometimes the phrases that flow from her keyboard are not those she would normally use, and she often experiences the emotions she is describing in her clients' lives. 'I'm a tool, a sort of catalyst for communication', she comments, 'So many people are tied to the physical and they need something tangible before they'll accept. With psychometry I can help them on a day-to-day basis.'

Sue is now beginning to move into a further, related area, that of remote viewing. Remote viewing has long been used by military departments in the United States, Russia and elsewhere to detect secret weapons facilities and to work out detailed maps of enemy territory. It is a very new skill to Sue, however, and she describes the sensation as akin to looking through someone else's eyes and seeing their environment. She believes she is being drawn to use her ability to uncover criminal activity, particularly violent assaults. The implications are enormous – imagine how helpful it would be to give police vital clues that enabled them to solve difficult cases.

The overwhelming desire to care for people is constant, but Sue hopes the physical support she expresses through nursing will give way to a deeper involvement in spiritual work. 'We're an average couple living in an average house with bills to pay,' she says simply. 'We're not religious, but we do feel in touch with whatever energy has created this complex planet, nature, geology, the human body, etc. And there are also minor energies that try to communicate. I'd now like to move on and learn much more about all of this.'

But Sue also states categorically: 'We don't have exclusive gifts or skills: anyone can do it. Many people expect thunder flashes and lightning bolts. But it's not usually like that. It's often the little things and looking properly at life around you that have the most to teach us. All the signs are out there, all the proof – you just have to find them. It's not going to be handed to you on a plate – what would the fun be in that?'

Stephen Cox and Gwyn Williams, psychic artists

How would you feel if a stranger sat down beside you and within thirty seconds sketched one of your relatives who had died some years previously? 'I don't believe it! Where's the catch?' might be a typical response, but there's no counterfeiting. Even though Steve Cox never meets most of the people he draws, he has a rare gift for capturing a person's absent friends and family with such uncanny accuracy that they are instantly recognisable. He is also able to portray what he feels are spirit guides whose expressions are so characterful that you cannot help but wonder who they are.

Even more incredible is that, with Steve's encouragement, his partner Gwyn is following his lead and is turning her hand to artwork of an unusual nature too. A young woman's face, surrounded by soft dark curls and with plump Cupid's bow lips thrusting upwards, reaches out from an A4 pad to greet me. 'That's one of Gwynnie's,' Steve declares proudly, 'Isn't she good?' I have to agree wholeheartedly.

We are relaxing in a large Victorian room. The view from the elegant windows is magnificent. I catch a glimpse of sparkling sea spray as broken lines of waves scurry towards the beach. It is Weston-super-Mare on a bright warm day in October, and I feel privileged to be invited into Steve's home, his private sanctuary. I'm told the house is also shelter to spirits from time to time. Only the other day a 'sweet little boy of about eight' dressed in 1950s school uniform – grey jumper, grey shorts, black shoes and grey socks pushed down to the ankles – knelt on Steve's bed for a full ten minutes…

If I were honest, I hadn't intended to speak to Steve about this book, because I'd already met his twin brother Martin, the animal healer. I'd decided at the outset that no one I interviewed should be related to anyone else I was writing about. But a series of quirky incidents led me on a direct path to Steve's front door. Before I pointed my finger at the bell, I had a hunch our chat would be intriguing and I wasn't disappointed. In hindsight, the only mild frustration was not to have met Gwyn, the talented hand behind an engaging array of portraits. Ironically, she was at art college that morning.

Steve does not look like his twin brother at all, although there is a great similarity in the way they speak and in their friendly exuberance. He feels very protective towards 'Marty', as 'we shared our mother's womb and were born together. We had a bond even in conception.'

I nudge him gently towards talking about his own life. How did he ever become what he terms a psychic artist? He goes back to his childhood to tease out the powerful threads that have been braided into the fabric of his personality.

'I remember my first psychic experience when I was about twelve' he begins confidently, 'I could read people, almost delve into them. I also felt there were lots of energies about me. At night I would lie there in bed and I would know there was something around me giving me peace and strength. It was a bit scary, but it was a fantastic feeling too. I didn't believe in God then, I couldn't understand where he was.

'Although our parents were non-religious and non-spiritual, they were both conscientious people and cared about what went on in the world. As well as bringing the four of us up (I have a strong, focused elder brother who's a reiki healer and musician, and a sister who makes documentaries for Channel 4 and who keeps me grounded), they would often welcome homeless people into the house. I remember we'd wake up in the morning and someone we didn't know would be in our front room.

'Dad also gave us lots of information – there was always a newspaper around – and he talked to us about everything. This compassionate atmosphere suited me. When I was six or seven I often daydreamed in school. I would imagine myself zooming across the sky like Superman and pinpointing those in trouble.

'At fourteen I have a distinct recollection of getting up in the morning and peering into the bathroom mirror. I saw three envelopes: one white and two brown. The next day these envelopes arrived for me. I thought, "Whoa! Hold on a minute here! What's going on?" I definitely felt some connection. As time passed, this sense of things being linked grew deeper and I realised there was a reason behind what was happening around me as a person.'

The opportunity to strengthen these connections between the physical and the ethereal came sooner than expected when Steve was a naive 17-year-old and was offered the chance to turn Superman dreams into reality. For a bit of fun he accompanied his brother Martin and their friends to a job interview. He had no inkling of what the position entailed except that there was a chance of travelling abroad. After the rest of the motley gang of teenagers had had their turn, a man popped his head round the door to the waiting room and asked if anybody else wished to talk to him.

After barely a second's thought, Steve offered himself and within a few minutes was bowled over with excitement at the prospect of becoming a care assistant with Voluntary Services Overseas (VSO). He was still part-way through 'A' levels, but was apathetic about completing them or even passing them if he stayed.

'I don't know who or what was pushing me into a caring profession so soon,' he says, 'but I do know I was being guided in some way. So it wasn't really surprising I was the sole person to be offered a job that day, even though I hadn't gone with the intention of applying for one!'

Steve never ceases to be amazed at how fearless he was when the wheels were set in motion straight away for him to leave school, home and country. He recalls: 'I was very green, very young and outgoing. I didn't know what I was letting myself in for, but there was a spiritual cloak around me, shielding me and propelling me onwards. I was lucky to have that.'

He adds thoughtfully, 'I do feel lucky in life – I'm an extraordinarily fortunate person. I just know I'm being guided to all these great things! I'm knocked down, like everyone else, but I get back up and continue stronger than ever before. As a psychic artist I have potentially hurtful comments aimed at me, because many people tell me I shouldn't communicate with the so-called dead. But why shouldn't we talk to our grandparents and why should we ever be frightened of dying?'

At this point Steve digresses to speak briefly about his current role as manager of a local hospice-owned nursing home. He is frequently moved by the plight of patients who approach death with monumental trepidation, and who 'hang on' desperately because they are terrified of what will happen to them.

'Religion has a lot to answer for,' he states dryly, 'and using the name of God to exert power over people throughout their lives is questionable. Very ill patients can become awfully anxious about things they've done and whether God is going to hammer them when they die. It's such a shame, as I'm sure we'll be fine when we go – though obviously we need to be aware of how we conduct ourselves in life, because I firmly believe that if you put good out you'll receive it back, and if you do bad you'll get that as well.'

After expressing his views on what I suppose comes under the heading of 'karma' (or, to be more precise, the spiritual law of cause and effect), he moves swiftly on to take up the reins again of his own case history. Following three enjoyable years with VSO in Germany, he returned to England where Martin found him a part-time job. A mutual acquaintance suggested he might like to visit a palmist. He was tempted, and warmed to the idea that somebody else might be able to discover information about him and his future. The experience proved slightly different from what he had imagined however.

'The lady gave me about five minutes, and the only comment of hers I can recollect is that I would have three letters after my name. This is the downside to such readings, because from then on it was scorched on my brain that I would have maybe only one set of qualifications. It could have prevented me from fulfilling my true potential, but I was determined not to allow it to hold me back and I've actually got about nine letters after my name now! In a way she wasn't exactly wrong and I wasn't put off from seeing some one like her again.

'Eventually, I decided to join some sort of spiritual group and cultivate whatever abilities I had. My network of contacts soon steered me in the right direction. About ten of us used to gather in a lady's front room each week – it wasn't a spiritualist church or anything like that, but a very strong, knowledgeable band of supportive people.'

Steve's first few sessions were pretty memorable. His friends greeted by name various spirits who would arrive in increasing numbers as the evenings wore on. Forgetting his earlier teenage episode with the three envelopes, he could not fathom how the others could see these entities, for he couldn't distinguish anything in the dimly-lit room beyond the usual chairs, curtains, lamps and his colleagues in meditative pose. In the fourth week, the situation altered abruptly and his learning curve shot upwards at pace.

A woman on his left-hand side was speaking about World War II when he suddenly found himself within the confines of an old aircraft's cockpit, struggling at the controls. 'A Spitfire or something similar came whooshing by and I was in the middle of a battle. I could see it all happening and I remember shouting out, "Wow! Look at that!"' says Steve animatedly. 'The lady and I were watching the same scene. We could describe what was going on and our accounts matched unequivocally.'

After this momentous incident, Steve knew his spiritual touchpaper had been well and truly lit. With encouragement from the group, his clairvoyance blossomed and he became a respected member. For some reason, perhaps because as a qualified pilot himself his main hobby is flying, he would often be

A portrait of Jonathon, a former RAF pilot and now one of Steve's spirit guides

contacted by spirit pilots (whom he now draws on a regular basis), and his face would take on the appearance of another person. Several times he contemplated allowing an RAF pilot, who was frequently present at the gatherings, to speak through him. But in the end he was not comfortable with the prospect and this is when his scribblings began.

Steve leaps up from his chair and bounds over to a table spread with precious examples of his work from the early days right up until what might have been merely a few hours ago.

'I kept getting information and I'd start to draw,' he explains and hurriedly extracts a couple of sheets of paper whose surface is bombarded with vigorous angular lines.

He continues, 'I would literally draw squiggles. They were just sketchy drawings of pure energy. Even though I'd passed 'O' level art and I'd set out to do an 'A' level, I'm not an artist really – though I'm becoming one with Gwyn's help – and I certainly couldn't draw faces. They were almost child-like when I was starting.'

To confirm his last statement he points to another picture: a roughly pencilled alien-looking visage looms up at me and I'm informed the name of this being is 'Aysha'. Several more less self-consciously drawn portraits of Aysha are placed reverently in front of me. The bold physiognomy and deep, luminous eyes are appealing in a strange way and I can indeed detect a growing assurance in the artist's work.

Another compare and contrast set is brought to the top of the pile, though in this case I learn that the male subject who appears in the two selected pictures was painted once by Steve and later by a fellow gifted artist who was not shown the original drawing. The similarities in both pictures are definitely there: large ruby lips, angular nose, youthful curly hair and, beyond the obvious physical features, that indefinable something which makes a person unique. Steve believes the man is his artist guide who lived during the 18th century in Scotland.

I am introduced next to an Edwardian gentleman whom Steve affectionately calls 'the navigator' and who has slightly wavy hair neatly parted down the centre of his head. Then there is a Native American with a spiky hairstyle, and an older man with a crucifix around his neck. Steve stops rifling through the portfolio to confide in me that whenever he needs to stand firm in an emotional sense 'the chap with the cross' is always close to him. A Buddhist monk is yet another member of his extended family of guides, but his presence is a mystery: 'I know he's here to help, but I don't know yet who he is or why he's with me.'

I assume that because Steve is working in such a visual medium he can see in his mind all the people he draws, but it seems this is absolutely not the case – which makes his results even

One of Gwyn's drawings of a spirit guide

The Cardinal – another of Steve's companions from the spirit world

more exceptional. 'I just get this feeling I have to draw,' he says simply, 'An energy comes to me and I can't focus on anything, even if I've got other work to do. I have to sit down and produce something. The only way I can explain the process is that I'm "impressed" upon. Gwyn does it quite differently, as she pictures the person. She can see the eyebrows or the hair.'

And then, smiling broadly, he adds, 'I'd always been told I'd work with my wife and I never thought it would happen. But since Gwyn and I met, I've come to realise she's my wife spiritually. She's only been doing this sort of thing for a year and already she's developed in leaps and bounds. At first she didn't think she'd be successful, but I persuaded her to have a go. She surprised herself and the outcome was this fantastic drawing. I could tell immediately it was a spirit person.'

I glance down at a further example of Gwyn's expertise. The perfect delineation of a handsome male profile is achieved with the minimum of effort. I am reminded of the smooth brush strokes in Japanese calligraphy.

Another oddity Steve describes in a matter of fact voice is that he never knows beforehand who he's going to draw, or whether they have died or are still alive. Even when he embarked on what transpired to be a picture of his own mother, who passed away some years ago, he did not realise it was her until he had virtually completed it. The choice of subject, it appears, is out of his hands: 'The guides and people select themselves. When Gwyn came to visit several years ago, I felt I had to pick up a piece of paper and a pencil. It took me about half a minute to make a caricature-type sketch of her grandfather, although I didn't know it was him or why I was doing it. She was staggered – I'd never met him! The fascinating thing is that if, say, I tried to draw you now, it wouldn't be half as good as if I were working in a psychic way.'

We move on to examples marking a pronounced change in Steve's work, almost as though he turned a sharp corner and shifted up a gear. They are more developed, the execution is more sophisticated. I'm shown a watercolour of a man in his sixties, dressed in the religious finery of a cardinal. Not only is the fuschia-pink habit striking, but the hooded eyes betray a hint of laughter which is echoed around the corners of the mouth where a faint mirthful twitch lingers. Steve agrees with my interpretation: this is a person with a grand sense of humour who probably enjoyed a guffaw or two with him in a previous life.

My attention is next drawn to a pastel portrait of a black person Steve calls Dominic. I glean this picture is of some significance to him, as it was born from three bleak days following the break-up of his marriage. The male face exudes poise and serenity, enough to dispel any torturous emotion. 'He's so beautiful,' sighs Steve, 'I do love my compositions.' I notice how once again he speaks devotedly of what to him are very real intimates in another dimension.

Like his subjects, the colours are 'felt' before they reach the paper. A butter yellow blouse on a middle-aged woman further sparks my imagination. I enquire whether he is given any feedback or confirmation of names from his models. The answer is spontaneous and direct: 'I usually sense an energy which tells me what I've done is right. Sometimes a name comes through, but not always.'

A Biggles-type pilot is propped up against the wall. He surveys the scene with solemn eyes. I can feel a tingling down my spine, so I turn, and there is the cardinal gazing at me from under half-closed lids.

'Here is someone's son who had died,' says Steve as he places an image of a young man in my hand. Now we're getting to the nub of his vocation: 'If I can help other people come to terms with their grief or just give them a bit of a lift, or maybe set them thinking about their life in a different way, then my gift of art is being put to the best use.'

Usually clients send him a photograph of themselves, but Steve can also use a letter or an e-mail to make a 'connection' with their spirit. To aid what in effect is long distance communication he may well bring in guidance from his runes from time to time too. With the assistance of a Japanese geisha guide, he then receives the crucial information which he manifests as a picture. And by tapping in to his mediumistic skills, he often 'channels' words of a personal nature for the recipient (but which are meaningless to him). The large package he eventually sends off to his clients is impressive.

Ever since Steve ventured into assisting people in this way, he has had only two negative responses, and one of those he believes was probably because of his keen insight into a private matter the individual was not facing up to.

He swerves away again from the main direction of our conversation and asks my opinion on what appears to be a Roman figure with a swathe of laurel leaves wrapped about his balding head. Then he veers back and, before I leave, makes a few more frank observations about some of the men and women who have contacted him.

'When I decided to advertise in *Psychic News*, I first had to prove my competence. They asked me to read off a photograph and apparently I drew someone's sister. Their response was so enthusiastic that I was over the moon. It's nice to have that sort of recognition, because it boosts you and gives you confidence. After that I had a lot of enquiries. One of my correspondents in Ireland turned out to be a clairvoyant. She was so pleased with the material I gave her that she put some of her own clients in touch with me, which means that I now have requests from the States and all over.

'I also get some very needy people asking for help. One German lady with many, many difficulties in her life has been writing every three to six months. I've felt obliged to deal with her letters, giving her past life information and such like. But I'm coming to the point where I feel I've done all I can for her and I must encourage her to try taking some responsibility for her own future. It would be very easy for her to become dependent on me, and that wouldn't be right at all.'

The time has flown by. We finish flicking through Gwyn's and Steve's files of portraits drawn for clients and in my admiration of their work I exclaim how the two of them are a force to be reckoned with. Steve flashes another of his happy smiles and prepares to go and meet Gwyn from college. Out of the corner of my eye, the cardinal is enjoying our banter. I'm almost convinced his lips are visibly trembling with suppressed laughter.

Neil Beechwood, numerologist and reiki master

Neil Beechwood has a strong affinity with Boscastle, a rugged step away along the cliffs from the bustle and drama of Tintagel. When I visited him, the cottage he'd lived in for the last three years reflected his calm and peaceful demeanour, with decorative embellishment limited to a few arresting *objets d'art* that splashed their bright colours against a simple pastel backdrop.

On first acquaintance, Neil is rather an enigma. What attracted someone, who readily admits to miserably failing his maths 'O' level, to leave a successful music career in London and devote himself to a discipline which calls for calculation and interpretation of numbers? It seems a contradiction in terms, but then Neil is a man for whom paradoxes are no stranger.

Speaking about the past, he confesses: 'All my life I'd felt like a round peg in a square hole, and it got to the point where things were so bad I hit rock bottom. When you reach that stage you start looking around for other sparks of interest, and that's when I came across numerology – divination by numbers.

'I'd been living in London for nine years and had enjoyed a reasonably prosperous time in the music industry. I was a promoter and used to arrange concerts, and I was also a singer/song writer in a group which received a lot of attention. But towards the end of my twenties and into my early thirties, I became bored, and very quickly over a period of about twelve months I changed considerably. The old patterns I'd grown accustomed to didn't appeal to me any more.

'One morning I was listening to the radio and a lady was on, promoting her book about numerology. She was inviting people to call in and have impromptu readings. The readings were so accurate that my imagination was really captured. I went straight out and bought a book of my own, read it avidly and then moved on to more in-depth study. After a while I found I actually had a talent for the subject, which was especially gratifying because at school my maths was poor – I'd make silly mistakes and then the whole sum would be wrong.

'I'd been deeply uninterested in arithmetic and dry numbers, but suddenly another world opened up for me: just as the brain has two sides – the rational and the intuitive – so I discovered that numbers can be looked at in different ways. And they can say something very significant about your life. My friends were soon convinced!'

According to Neil, Pythagoras is thought of as the modern father of numerology. While the word 'modern' might appear to be another of those incongruities, Pythagoras's accounts apparently refer to 'the ancients' – the Chaldeans, Assyrians, Babylonians, Egyptians – who each had their own version of what in essence is the same system employed today.

Since the demise of those early great civilisations, it's probably true to say that numerology continued to bubble away in the background, practised by a few enthusiasts worldwide. But in more recent times it wasn't until the nineteenth century when the increasingly influential Theosophical Society brought old teachings out into the open once more that it regained its popularity. Nobody knew how it worked, just that it did. From then on it went from strength to strength.

Neil willingly explains the principles, though it soon becomes clear that he is merely skimming the surface of what is at once an impressively detailed method of observing a person's character and yet, for the skilled practitioner, a very simple one too.

He describes a reading as like taking a two-dimensional black and white, grainy snap shot. In a similar way to astrology, it pinpoints potential, your psychic make-up and how your life, in general terms, will pan out.

'If you're aware of your strengths and weaknesses, it can be a great help,' states Neil. 'So many of us are trying to be like somebody else, like our role models. That's fine if our heroes and

The beautiful harbour of Boscastle where Neil felt drawn to find a new home

heroines are quality people, but we really need to acknowledge who *we* truly are. And this is where a proficient numerologist comes in.

'If you have a reading from someone who doesn't know you, merely by doing a few sums they can say pretty accurately, "This is what you're good at, this is what you're going through at the moment, when you were 15 something like this happened to you, you're motivated by *x*, you love *y*, but you don't like *z*!"

'For anyone who is serious about getting to the bottom of themselves, numerology is an excellent tool. It enables you to take stock of yourself. But I have to admit that too many people treat it as entertainment. They have a gap in their life and want to fill it, but after they've had a consultation they simply go away and never reflect on the important information they've been given.'

To provide a clearer idea of the scope of Neil's craft, here is a distillation of what he revealed.

Every letter within the alphabet is ascribed a number, so A = 1, B =2, C = 3 and so on. When double figures are reached, the total of the two digits added together is then reduced to one figure. For example, **J** = 10 = **1** (1 + 0); **M** = 13 = **4** (1 + 3); **P** = 16 = **7** (1 + 6); **Y** = 25 = **7** (2 + 5).

In other words, the core of numerology is based on numbers 1 to 9, and can be applied to the names of people, pets, places, houses, towns – anything which has a name and on which you feel a reading might shed some light. It can also be used on telephone numbers, car registrations, dates of birth and house numbers: the limit is your imagination.

The exception to the rule of reducing down to a single digit is when what is called a 'master number' – 11 or 22 – is reached (some numerologists affirm that every double number – 11, 22, 33, 44, 55 etc – is a master number).

For some inexplicable reason borne out through hundreds of thousands of readings, these two master numbers have a particular resonance and so they are not reduced to 2 and 4 respectively. It would seem that individuals with either or both of them in their chart, perhaps as the day on which they were born, feel set apart from others, and they experience a great deal of tension in their lives. They have the capacity to follow a very spiritual path and in that respect could be construed as 'distinctive' in some way but, in Neil's words, 'There's no such thing as a free lunch!' – they have to work hard at achieving harmony and non-material success.

Returning to numbers 1 to 9, Neil has his own logical interpretation of each one within the sequence, but is also quick to point out that the process is not as clear cut as might at first appear.

For example, while several people might all be '3s', perhaps as a result of arriving at 12, 21 or 30 in their computations, their individuality would be disclosed by their original compound number which is special in its own right. Someone with 21, for instance, would primarily be a 3 person, but would also exhibit characteristics of a 2 and to a lesser degree of a 1.

And so to Neil's definition of every number's ideal points, starting with 1. Remember that each has an essence of the one immediately before and after it (9 is followed by 1). Bear in mind too that the numbers also have under- and over-balanced energies. For example, an over-balanced 1 energy is dominating, bossy and arrogant, whereas an under-balanced 1 energy is sly and lacking motivation.

1

1 is the yang or masculine number that begins the whole cycle. If you're a 1 person, you're generally confident, a strong leader and normally unafraid to stand up in front of others. You're not frightened by responsibility and you like taking projects on, but you're not as good at carrying them through to fruition.

2

This is the yin or feminine number, and represents togetherness and co-operation. 2 people are excellent listeners, but are not keen at speaking publicly. They much prefer to be the power behind the throne, a role they play extremely well.

3

The product of a man's and a woman's relationship is often a baby, and so 3 is the number of creativity and joy. If you're a 3 person you're resourceful, very friendly, love being around people and enjoy the world to the full.

4

After the baby has been born it's time to put down foundations and this is where 4, the number of work, discipline, organisation and practicality comes in – if you think about it, a four-sided figure such as a square or cube placed on the floor is certainly solid and grounded.

5

5 people tend to be accomplished in many different spheres and have to be careful not to vacillate too much between one task and another. Interested in a wide range of topics, they may be jack of all trades and master of none. But on a positive note, they are splendid communicators, and love travel and freedom.

6

6 is the number of devotion, harmony, balance and service. In tarot it is represented by the lovers, which can indicate higher as well as physical love. 6 is also connected with caring in the home, family or close community.

Having ascended, in metaphorical terms, almost to the summit of earthly life, the next three, or 'higher', numbers in the sequence move on to look at other aspects of existence.

7

In India an old tradition once prevailed where, as soon as a man's children had left home or his wife had died, he would become a 'sadhu', a type of wandering monk. Even though he might have been a wealthy businessman or a judge or a politician, he would forsake all his material gains in a search for greater truths. 7, therefore, represents analysis and understanding on the one hand and intuition on the other – you're high up on that mountain meditating! You're very much centred around your mind and brain, and being on your own is important to you. You might also feel as though you're on a different wavelength from everybody else.

8

8 is a powerful number of action and accomplishment. It can encompass acquisition of money, but it really embraces much more than that: similar in some ways to 1s, 8 people are effective managers and natural bosses whose colleagues enjoy working for them because they are so inspirational.

9

Being the highest number in the cycle, 9 reflects selflessness and humanitarianism. 9 people are generous and caring, but since their psychic make-up draws others to them for help they may find they are continually giving of themselves, often with little thanks in return. For this reason numerology recognises there are more mentally negative 9s than any other number! It takes a distinctive sort of person to be completely unselfish and to provide willingly time and time again without expecting anything in return.

One of the basic principles of numerology is that, in the same way as the earth has cycles throughout the seasons, months, weeks and days, so numbers have their own rhythmic patterns. Take, for example, your year number.

To discover what this is, first look at your day of birth. If there are two numbers, add them together and reduce to a single digit or a master number. Next, do the same for the month and add this to the day digit, again reducing to a single figure. Then repeat the process for the year until you are left with one digit or a master number.

If at the end of the sums you have, say, a 9, then you were born into a 9 year and that is your life path. On your second birthday, numerologically speaking you entered your personal year 1 of a 9-year cycle, and your experiences would reflect the 1 accordingly. For another person in year 1 of perhaps an 8 cycle, the general influences would be the same, but the way they dealt with them, how their individual energy responded to that year, would be different from yours.

Once you start trying to unravel these complexities, it soon becomes obvious that an expert's insight is essential for drawing out the subtleties in your personal chart.

It is widely agreed that a computer is not an acceptable substitute for consulting a professional, as a mechanical reading will often highlight many different 'aspects' which seem to contradict one another (an aspect describes a particular facet of a person's character). One moment you're being told you're an outgoing individual, and the next that you're a loner!

A capable practitioner, in contrast, will take the various calculations from your date of birth and/or your name and will present you with a coherent report based on an understanding of *all* the data – for instance the total number of vowels in a name mean one thing, consonants another, and yet more can be deduced from the amount of 1s, 2s, 3s etc. And then there are what Neil terms 'expressions'. These indicate how a subject expresses themselves through their abilities, what their motivation is at a deep soul level – regardless of what they think they want on a conscious level – and how they like to be viewed by other people. In fact the permutations seem infinite.

At this point Neil's lively face, eyes shining and vibrant, displays his infectious passion for the ancient art he came across by chance on a crackly radio station one gloomy morning several years ago.

After a few more questions, however, it is evident that he has a further piece of 'magic' up his sleeve, another hugely motivating force in his life which he describes as 'something incredibly profound, like numerology, that you don't have to study'. Its name? Reiki.

Neil gives a quick background *résumé*. Reiki, meaning 'universal life energy', was developed at the end of the nineteenth century in Japan by a man called Dr Mikao Usui (1865-1926). Dr Usui was interested in different spiritual perspectives, and would often go off on retreat and meditate.

On one such occasion, while standing near a waterfall on Mount Kurama, he had an exceptionally potent experience that left him with the ability to heal. Not only this, he knew he had also accessed the means of empowering other people to do the same.

After his dramatic enlightenment he called the system of healing 'reiki', and went on to found a society which set up centres throughout Japan. Treatments by Dr Usui and his colleagues helped large numbers of patients, including people injured by the devastating Tokyo earthquake in 1923.

Little else is known about Dr Usui – information passed on by Hawayo Takata, a Japanese-American lady who brought reiki to the West, has recently been researched and found to be untrue. It's likely that Hawayo Takata changed the origin story to make reiki more acceptable, but whatever her motives she was successful at introducing an extraordinary spiritual gift to different cultures.

Today, thanks mainly to Frank Arjava Petter, a modern reiki master and author, the practice of reiki in its modern forms is thriving more than ever before.

'Reiki differs from what I'd call traditional spiritual healing,' claims Neil, 'in that anyone who's been initiated can do it. You don't have to study for it or have any particular knowledge or belief.

'The initiation is a form of spiritual ceremony during which there's a transference of energy from the teacher to the student. Like numerology, we don't know exactly how it works, and from what I've read Dr Usui did not fully understand the science behind it either. The four higher chakras [chakras are like spinning vortices of energy at various points along the body] are involved – that's the crown, third eye, throat and heart.

'During the first initiation these chakras are opened more than usual. This makes them more effective at drawing in the universal life energy which surrounds us all the time and is the "ki" part of reiki – "rei" means "universal". Some people also refer to it as "prana" or "chi" and it's the most fundamental life-giving source. There are other sources, such as the sun, the air we breathe, water and food, but these are not directly tapped into for reiki healing.

'After the initiation you don't have to visualise anything. And because you're just a conduit for what can only ever be good energy, it doesn't really matter what you say – though many reiki masters might disagree. I always remember Hawayo

Takata's words: "Hands on, reiki on!" You just put your hands there and the energy comes through. Takata wanted to maintain the simplicity which she felt was so important for everyday life. But if any student wishes to express themselves in some positive way before or while giving healing, then I would encourage them to do so.

'Another point to mention about starting reiki is that, because all of a sudden you have access to a new level of energy, people often experience what's called a cleansing process or healing crisis which lasts for three weeks. Each of the seven main chakras is purified in turn, starting with the root on day 1, the sacral on day 2, the solar plexus on day 3, and so on. The process happens three times, and can provoke weird dreams, high emotions, and the release of toxins through the skin which can make you spotty! Sometimes nothing occurs and then people may feel disappointed!'

Neil continues by describing the three levels or degrees in reiki, each of which involves an initiation and is ideally carried out on separate occasions. After the first, students can try healing friends, family, pets, even plants, but the most intriguing aspect is that an individual can actually work on themselves.

As Neil says, 'It really is a question of "Physician, heal thyself!"' He expresses the view that if everyone were introduced to reiki, there would be incalculable benefits across the planet. 'You don't even have to think about it as a spiritual thing,' he maintains, 'You might feel a cold coming on and simply put your hands on your throat.'

I ask Neil whether regular practice is necessary. His answer is typically informative and fascinating: 'Once you've had the initiation, theoretically you could forget about reiki for fifty or sixty years, go back to it and it would still be there for you. Having said that, the more you work at it, the better it is – although at first degree level there is a limit to how much you can achieve, and this is why many people feel they wish to move on.

'When you're giving healing or receiving it yourself, the energy first comes into the crown chakra, then flows through the third eye, throat and heart chakras. It then flows down the arms through subtle energy channels or meridians and out through the chakras in the hands. Just as blood arteries can become clogged, so the subtle channels can be blocked through non-use. Regular healing keeps the channels clear. So practice is definitely advisable!'

The second degree, for which Neil recommends waiting a minimum of three months after the first, is called the practitioner level and enables you to draw on more energy. As a result you are better equipped to treat others. You also receive a set of symbols, each of which is a key to a specific quality of the energy and can be invoked under particular circumstances, for example when someone is emotionally upset or depressed.

'We now have symbols for balancing, grounding and protection,' explains Neil, 'because often in healing there's a slight concern about contracting an illness from a patient, which is certainly possible. There's also a symbol for distant healing, but I actually teach first level students to send healing to people or animals they can't physically touch – and it seems to be equally effective. Perhaps there will come a time when we don't need these emblems at all, where when we think something it will happen automatically. I feel we're moving in that direction already.'

The third stage or instructor level is the master degree. Many people are uncomfortable with the title of master, as masters in other disciplines generally spend years devoted to learning and understanding. A reiki mastership, on the other hand, is conferred on someone as soon as they have received the initiation, which might be anywhere between one and five years, and certainly at least six months, after the second degree.

However, Neil stresses that teachers are born and not made, and advises prospective students to question masters about their courses. For him, there was no question about his route forward: 'I knew after the second degree that I'd come across something so awe-inspiring, so dear to me, that I just had to go out and offer it to others.'

At this point Neil deviates slightly to comment on how a patient feels when receiving healing. His initial statement is 'Wonderful!', but then in more serious vein he describes a range of what to many may seem very strange experiences. 'I use reiki-seichem, a system which contains what you might call sub-sets of energy and these produce varying sensations such as warmth, fierce heat, tingling, coolness, icy cold, even breezes over the body. There are also times when you know the healer's hands are on your head but it feels as though someone is touching your feet. That is very bizarre when you're aware someone is working on you and yet no one's there.

'Pain can disappear almost instantaneously, but it would be unwise to say a particular ailment will always respond in a particular way in any given number of healing sessions. Reiki does not cure anything. What it does do is empower the immune system and all the other physical and emotional systems in the body. For that reason it is the ultimate holistic treatment: with more energy at its disposal, the body requires less time to mend itself. Patients typically feel greatly soothed and much calmer after a reiki session.'

Neil's admiration for Dr Usui and his reverence of what befell this ordinary Japanese businessman in the late 1800s have inspired him to conduct student initiations at the foot of St Nectan's Glen waterfall near Tintagel: 'It's a powerful, peaceful place and mirrors Dr Usui's experience, which makes the whole occasion so memorable and evocative for everyone concerned. That's not to say it can't be done elsewhere. I run courses in London on a busy bus route and the ability of the healers there is the same as those fortunate enough to walk up through the Glen. But given the choice, I would opt for St Nectan's every time.'

This empathy between Neil and his Cornish surroundings is

almost palpable. As a child he often holidayed in North Devon – Croyde and Woolacombe – and occasionally he and his family ventured further south into Cornwall. He recalls that when he was fourteen he came to Boscastle and was deeply influenced by the place and its atmosphere. At the time he never put into words what he felt, but the impact was such that in his heart there was always a pull to return.

'After I'd had enough of London,' he reminisces, 'I went to the Himalayas for six months. I gave up my flat and put everything into storage. When I came back I had very little money. The plan was to buy a cheap car, drive towards the west and find somewhere to live. I went through all sorts of places, including Glastonbury and Lyme Regis, on the way down, but I was drawn like a magnet to Boscastle. At first nothing was available there, so I stayed in Tintagel youth hostel for a while and then took a bedsit. I would often walk my landlord's dogs along the cliffs and dream of moving to Boscastle – it felt so right for me.

'One day I picked up the local paper and in the box ads was a cheap, one-bedroom cottage in the village. I called the landlord, got on well with him and moved in straight away. Since then I've enjoyed the challenges Cornwall has to offer. Many spiritual people are drawn here, but it can be frustrating if you can't work in the way you'd like to – I myself eke out a living based in Boscastle, but I have to travel to London to expand my business. I may have to make that a more permanent arrangement.'

Neil sums up by saying, 'There are amazing energies in the West Country, some dynamic and positive and others, such as those around underground streams, potentially stress-inducing. Because of this, Cornwall can be a challenging place to live. You can be here a couple of years and be in the beauty of it and that can sustain you, but after a while you have to face yourself big time – and in that respect it's a fantastic place to follow a spiritual life…'

Lynne Orchard, guardian of a sacred site

Glastonbury, ancient mystical Isle of Avalon, is like a precious lodestone for modern pilgrims and spiritual seekers who, following the rhythm of the seasons, converge on its streets and cluster like brilliantly dabbed butterflies in the surrounding countryside. It is a meeting point for different faiths, a venue that encourages creative self-expression and, for those open to its vibrations, a potential catalyst for change. Although not all are moved to the same degree, mention its name and for most people Glastonbury will resonate in some way.

Just outside the town centre, in Chilkwell Street, is a Somerset jewel. A breath away from the road, the full extent and beauty of the Chalice Well gardens gradually unfold as you saunter along the paths among the trees and foliage. There is a subtly enveloping, protective atmosphere which somehow triggers inner reflection. In spring and summer, flowers trumpet their striking colours, while at other times the gardens' personality is conveyed through muted hues and rustling twigs. And always at the heart there is the flow of water, rising up from the sacred spring and spilling down through troughs and pools.

Lynne Orchard and her husband Michael, who for many years were drawn to Chalice Well simply to enjoy the tranquillity, were chosen as its 'guardians' by the site's own spiritual energies. Their job, or 'service' as they prefer to view it, is almost certainly unique, for it's unlikely that any other similarly regarded location in the country is run in quite the same way.

Like the custodians before them, they manage all aspects of the environment, from looking after visitors and overseeing staff to listening to the gardens and focusing attention wherever it is needed. While currently relishing the challenges offered, they firmly believe that, just as they were called by Chalice Well, when the time is right it will also reveal when they should leave.

The route which brought them here is fascinating. Over twenty years ago Michael hitchhiked a lift to Glastonbury and was dropped off at Chalice Well. The then guardian happened to be around when he climbed out of the vehicle and plopped his belongings onto the ground. He welcomed him in and invited him to peer down the well into the water.

Michael did not know where he was being escorted, and was even more nonplussed when, with his head part way down the well head, the guardian asked him to consider who he, Michael, was! Far from being alienated by this experience, he felt an instant attraction to Chalice Well and visited whenever he could.

Lynne's introduction was less dramatic but left just as deep an impression. She arranged with a friend to meet outside the entrance, although she didn't know where or what Chalice Well was. Later on, after satisfying her curiosity with a pleasant wander round the gardens, which were in spectacular full bloom, she became instantly hooked and knew deep inside that one day she would be intimately linked with them in some way. It was twelve years before her premonition proved correct.

When Lynne and Michael eventually met each other, they therefore already shared a common bond. And as both had such an affinity with the Well, it seemed the most natural place in the world for them to arrange their 'hand-fasting' ceremony when, some years later, they wanted to celebrate their relationship. It also gave respite when planning different phases in their working lives; they would relax in the quietness, mulling over the choices ahead of them. The gardens always provided them with the much needed serenity and clarity they sought.

Being such frequent visitors, they became friendly with the resident guardians who hinted they should consider taking over their mantle. Although hugely flattered, they never really paid much attention as they were busy leading their own lives. Eventually, however, they were informed the guardians were intent on leaving and that they should apply for the positions.

The Lion's Head, where spring water can be drunk

They duly did so, though when it came to the crunch they opted to take a year off and devote it to their personal spiritual development.

Under the new guardianship the Well flourished but, in time, due to personal problems the guardians felt unable to continue. At this point a trustee serendipitously picked up a piece of paper from a desk in the office, turned it over and found, to her great delight, the letter Lynne and Michael had written three years previously.

As the trustee made the phone call to invite them over, Lynne and Michael were about to close a deal to run a new set of training courses. Fortunately, they had not signed on the dotted line and, sensing it was now the appropriate time to commit themselves to Chalice Well, responded enthusiastically. These peculiar circumstances which led them here are why they feel that, when the right people are ready to assume the responsibilities of where it wishes to go, the Well calls to it those it needs.

Catching Lynne on an exceptionally busy day, she steals half an hour from her hectic schedule to convey a flavour of this secluded treasure. We enter a beautiful, airy meeting room which has a high ceiling and spears of natural daylight penetrating the elevated windows. A hallowed ambience curls round us as we position two chairs in the middle of a large red carpet and then settle ourselves to talk.

Lynne begins by running through some of the historical background, though points out that, while she can retain detailed information about other places, at Chalice Well it's as though she is 'not allowed to' in case she side-steps current issues – her role is to concentrate on the present, to be alert constantly to what is going on around her.

She speaks softly and with the utmost respect for what has become her home: 'Chalice Well is known as a sacred site because of its unending supply of water from a primary spring deep underground. We take it so much for granted that when we turn a tap on we'll get as much instant water as we want, but for thousands of years people recognised the enormous importance of this constant life-giving source and offered their thanks and blessings to the springs.

'Just sitting next to the water as it bubbles up, and listening to the sound, connects you deep within. It relaxes your body and mind, and draws you into an inner silence. As you sit quietly, the waters reflect back to you your experiences and your needs, giving you time to contemplate them away from everyday life.

'People have been making pilgrimages to Chalice Well for generations; they come for purification, baptism, rites of passage, and healing. The curative power of the waters can be traced back to the mid-18th century when a certain Matthew Chancellor published an account of a dream in which he was directed to drink a glass of the waters on seven successive Sunday mornings. He followed these instructions and found himself cured! This healing then drew crowds of people from the surrounding countryside, all seeking cures for their own ailments.

'Today you can drink the iron-enriched water, which stains the basin red, from the "Lion's Head". And at "Arthur's Court" you can put your hands into it by the "Pilgrim's Pool", or you can bathe your feet – but be careful of the pool's slippery bottom or you may find yourself fully immersed!'

With such a firmly established focal point for the community, it is fortunate that in its more recent history a few enlightened individuals had the foresight to secure its future by taking action at key moments. Alice Buckton, who ran the Well from 1912 to the mid 1940s, recognised its vital connection with the surrounding scenery and purchased land, including two thirds of Chalice Hill, to protect it from potential building threats.

After Alice Buckton, Wellesley Tudor Pole, another visionary who knew and treasured the area, made a huge impact during his tenure. In 1959 he set up a Charitable Trust which in turn appointed guardians who, according to Lynne, have always been and always will be deeply committed to the Well. The

Trust is now self-supporting by its entrance fees, small book-shop, Companions (who are friends of the Well), and by donations and legacies. The Companions live all over the world, each having a particular attachment to Chalice Well after being touched by its timeless, restorative qualities.

Lynne picks up the thread again: 'There has always been a spring on this site and the gardens have grown up around the waters to create this beautiful place. In the early years Wellesley Tudor Pole, together with the help of many sympathetic volunteers who wished to conserve it for the future, transformed it into what you see today.

'The gardens evolved gradually, with people bringing plants from their own gardens. It seems that right from the beginning all who have come here have felt the love, peace and generosity of spirit that have been imprinted on the earth.

'Today the same values and sense of sacredness exist in everyone who works at Chalice Well, each receiving whatever they need from the place. They are always listening to what the land, plants and elementals have to say. Nothing is planted, moved or changed without first asking and being aware of the subtle energies that exist within the garden – we are working together as co-creators. The gardeners use only organic methods, so it is a safe environment for the wildlife.'

Lynne then adds, thoughtfully, 'The garden is full of nature spirits. If you sit quietly and ask with an open heart, you can usually feel their presence. It may take time, but you just need to keep trying. Some people actually see them, but others sense their company.

'The garden has different moods, too, which are often indicative of your own. It brings you back into balance and surrounds you with a loving embrace. I find great solace if I'm at a low ebb, anxious or out of harmony. I usually walk between the guardian yew trees, and I will feel their spirits talk to me and a still calmness move through me. This can also happen in other parts of the garden – each person finds their own special place when they visit and has their own unique experience.

'That is why as a guardian I need to be as receptive as I can to all – we try to honour the spirit of each individual. People often come when they are distraught, and they seem to find comfort in the garden which they cannot find elsewhere. Chalice Well is a natural temple within the landscape and many are drawn to it for the profound peace it can bring them.'

We next turn our thoughts to the powerful Vesica Piscis symbol (two interlocking circles) which has a strong presence in the gardens. It embellishes the wrought iron lid that covers the well head, forms part of the footpath leading to the entrance and beyond, and is reproduced to great effect in the Vesica Pool at the lower end of the gardens. I learn from Lynne that this particular design was taken from a 13th-century pattern and represents the Bleeding Lance holding in balance the visible and invisible worlds interlocked with each other. She comments, 'The symbol shows us that one of the experiences of Chalice Well is about the union of Earth and Spirit. As we become more aware, we realise there is no separation between the two.'

After a few seconds' silence, Lynne has a few more insightful comments about the symbolism in the gardens, 'We welcome people from every religion, although there are strong links here to Christianity, Celtic Spirituality and the Goddess – we celebrate the Christian and Celtic festivals as much as we can. A lot of men and women are also drawn to Chalice Well because of the strong feminine energy that flows from it – here they connect with the female essence.

'The waters symbolise the potential for creation of new life in the form of new ideas, inspirations or projects. And next to the Chalice Well flows the White Spring, representing the male energy. Within the gardens you can see the red and white reflected in the berries and the fruits of the Holy Thorn trees. One day the Red and White Springs may flow together again as they probably once did in ancient times.'

I am conscious of the clock so, reluctantly, we move away

from the subject of the gardens to talk quickly about the fifteenth-century Little St Michael's Retreat House and the Meeting room, which is another integral feature of Chalice Well. There are six bedrooms and self-catering facilities and, according to Lynne, Companions are able to rest here and take time out to enjoy the soothing atmosphere. And sometimes groups of a spiritual or healing nature rent the facilities for their own events, taking full advantage of the house's beauty and relishing the availabilility of the gardens after opening hours – this, for many, makes their stay particularly special.

Lynne rationalises the attraction: 'A lot of people, myself included, take the feel of a place to heart. The more time you spend here, the more it seeps into your whole structure so that when you need to call on it, it's there for you and gives you strength. It's very difficult to explain because it's not tangible, but it is one of the gardens' great treasures. That's why people come back constantly to replenish. You may be sitting in your flat in the middle of a busy city, but you can still recall the calmness you felt at Chalice Well. You can then cope with whatever you need to do with more ease. This ancient place is a haven for us all in our busy, hectic lives.'

The sun must be dipping low on the horizon, for I detect a dimming of light in the room. I put one last question to Lynne: does she feel honoured to have been chosen to be a guardian of Chalice Well? 'Yes, of course,' she replies, 'I'm still in love with Chalice Well, years after first visiting. But every being meets what it needs to challenge it, and we've obviously reached that point in life where the challenges here are what we need to learn from.

'It's no different from any one else's journey – it's just a different situation. It's always important to remember these things, to keep grounded and not let your ego become inflated. Glastonbury has the kind of energy that can spin you up and throw you about, and it can be very unsettling – like being in a cauldron! But it can also be transformational!'

Janet Gay, clairvoyant, and David Gay, healer and trance medium

If you'd said ten years ago to Janet and David Gay, a happily married couple living and working in Bodmin, that within 18 months their lives would be transformed beyond all recognition they would have laughed you out of the room.

They were reasonably content just as they were: David, a psychiatric nurse at the local hospital, was coping with the odd hours his shifts imposed on him and, although Janet was beginning to have serious problems with arthritis, she was enjoying her nursing assistant job there too. With plenty of family and friends nearby, they were satisfied with what the world had thrown at them. They could never have conceived in a million years just what was in store the day they pulled up in the pouring rain outside a spiritualist church.

Janet's mother and father were both spiritualists and went to a local church in London, so Janet grew up believing in spirits but never really seeing or hearing them. She knew that if she asked for help it would come from intangible forces, even though she couldn't quite comprehend how or why. David, on the other hand, a local Cornishman who can trace his ancestors back to copper mining days, was a determined atheist. As Janet now wryly comments, he thought anything to do with spiritual matters 'complete rubbish'.

One wet and blustery evening, Janet's mother asked on the spur of the moment if she could go to a spiritualist church. Janet offered to accompany her, and David reluctantly agreed to drive them there. But he had absolutely no intention of going into the building – he would wait outside. When he stopped the car, however, the wind was sweeping leaves up into the darkened sky and heavy showers were deluging the road. He soon had second thoughts and opted for the warmth and light of the nearby hall where the service was being held.

Once inside, he was in for a terrific shock. The presiding medium almost immediately gave him a message whose content was so relevant and personal that he could not disagree with it. His instinctive reaction was to turn to his wife and insist she reveal to him how she had conveyed all this private information. But as Janet pointed out, they hadn't known they were going to the church until half an hour or so beforehand and she certainly was not familiar with the woman.

Six months later David found himself inside a church rather unwillingly for the second time. Yet again he was presented with persuasive evidence, although on this occasion it came via a different medium. He was told a man dressed in army uniform wished to contact him – someone of whom he had just one photograph.

The realisation slowly dawned on him: his mother had died three weeks after his birth and his father, upset and heavily involved in military life, placed the children into foster care. David was brought up by his aunt and never saw his father again. The only proof he ever possessed of his parent's existence was a single black and white print of a handsome young soldier. And it was indeed propped up at home.

Several more months elapsed before he received a startling third message. Janet had for a while shown a vague interest in crystals and this had now developed into a keen enthusiasm. On a friend's recommendation she decided to visit a local shop to buy a few crystals of her own. She and David searched at length for the place, but the name of the road they had been given did not present any stores at all. However it did yield another spiritualist church and yet another medium!

Feeling compelled to attend a service after discovering the church in such an unusual manner, they returned that same evening. Their jaws plummeted when they were informed that they would both become mediums and that one day David, a budding healer, would open his own church.

As Janet says, 'It was one thing for me to believe in life after death, but quite another to be told about my future mediumship.'

After receiving the stunning news, they both agreed to brave the church again. Every time they ventured to a service David was always given a message by a different person, but there was rarely anything for Janet who suggests, 'I was already believing so "they", the spirits, had to keep getting at him to hook him!'

Eventually David capitulated: having had more unexplained communications about mediumship and healing than he cared to count, he resolved to put his untried talents to the test. Each night for the next three weeks Janet received the benefit of his ministrations, and she can now recall that 'even though the arthritis was still there, the pain was much less and I had greater mobility. We actually saw a huge improvement'.

Due to the severe condition of her back, she had been advised by doctors that she would end up in a wheelchair if she continued full-time work. Now, although the disease had not disappeared totally, her walking was better. This was a remarkable turn of events, and both felt a little awed by the exciting, but also daunting situation they seemed to be moving towards.

'It does make you wonder why these things happen,' she ponders, 'If I hadn't had the arthritis and I'd been working full-time, I wouldn't have been able to develop my spiritual gifts.'

After that they were next bombarded with messages about the need to sit in a development circle. They had no idea what this was, but knew from recent adventures they should soon find out. With guidance from members of the church and after an invigorating week spent at the Spiritualists' National Union (SNU) college at Stansted Hall in Essex, they began to make sense of their odd experiences.

Janet had often wondered whether the colourful domestic scenes she saw during meditation – people gardening…standing at a gate and gossiping with one another…busy cooking in a kitchen – were the product of an over-fertile imagination. But she was soon convinced otherwise.

The belief that it was spirit people she was glimpsing seemed to be verified when she and David worked by themselves at home. She could describe his old patients, his nursing colleagues, next door neighbours he knew as a child, and members of his vast family. In short, she described people whom only David had come into contact with or, in the case of his relatives, whose names would be confirmed later when the family tree was researched.

About the same time they began to make progress with their mediumship, mischievous activity started up within the house. Janet recounts the strange episodes involving invisible entities: 'Objects were moved around or would disappear only to reappear six months later. Books would fall off the bookcase, but not just straight down on to the floor as you'd expect: they'd end up on the other side of the room! We saw things literally flying through the air. And we'd be touched, but when we turned around nobody would be there.'

Undeterred by all these bizarre incidents, David and Janet reached the point in their training when they were ready for their 'fledgling' evening at church. Apparently at such evenings the congregation is aware that mediums are making their first appearance, but even a sympathetic audience cannot always dispel nerves.

Janet remembers her early anxiousness: 'In the beginning I used to shake like a leaf, my hands used to sweat buckets and my mouth was as dry as a bone. It was extremely nerve-wracking, but I felt it was something I had to do, my purpose in life. I still get quivery and feel sick before a service, but once I'm working within Spirit energy I'm not aware of my own aches and pains; my arthritis vanishes – until afterwards when my body then lets me know I've been on my feet a long time!'

Just one month later, on the day of their wedding anniversary, they were chosen to officiate at their first service proper. Janet is amused when I ask whether people sat around in a shadowy room waiting to hear spectral table-raps. The images conjured

up by the word 'seance', which to some people is synonymous with 'spiritualist', seem comical to her: 'Spiritualist churches are not like that at all. We sing hymns, have prayers and readings, listen to inspirational talks and discuss philosophy, as well as have some time for communication with the spirit world. The exception is when there's a so-called "evening of clairvoyance" which is devoted wholly to message giving by an invited medium.'

At this point David interrupts briefly to explain the terminology. 'We always advertise evenings of clairvoyance, because that's what people understand, but sometimes when you get there it turns out the medium isn't clairvoyant at all! If you listen carefully to what they say, you can work out how they're in touch with the spirits.

'If they talk about a person *showing* them something, it does indeed mean they're clairvoyant. But if they say this person is *telling* them, it usually indicates they're clairaudient, while if they use the expression "I *feel* Mrs S is wearing such and such", it probably means they're clairsentient. I don't see or hear, but I do sense the spirit people. I can still describe the colour of a dress, an individual's personality – whether they are sad or bossy – just by how I feel. It's as accurate as the other ways, if not more so.'

Now that they had well and truly dipped their toes into the water, they were thrilled to receive invitations to attend other churches in the area. Fortunately, David's working regime changed quite dramatically at this point.

Up till then he had managed to juggle his spiritual develop-ment with the emotionally and physically demanding shifts at the hospital. But he was aware that the time was soon approaching when he would have to curtail his non-nursing activities. As luck would have it, this course of action was avoid-ed when he was moved on to a conventional 5-day week.

The coincidence did not go unnoticed: finishing at 5 o'clock each day meant that his evenings were freed, enabling him to make an even greater commitment to spiritual disciplines.

Since then this dedication to their craft and their desire to improve the quality of mediumship nationally have become an integral part of David's and Janet's lives. 'People will go to the college for a week', Janet bemoans, 'and come back and say "I'm a medium!", but a week just throws up lots of areas for improvement.

'So many are involved in earning a living and getting by on instant meals that they want instant mediumship as well. It's not enough – you have to give time and commitment. In fact, if I'd known beforehand about all the responsibilities that go with the territory, I'd never have embarked on it! It's quite ironic that genuine mediums aren't recognised by the law, only the fraud-ulent ones!'

According to Janet, responsibilities and skills range from adhering to strict codes of conduct to understanding and being honest with yourself, creating a strong link with the spirit world and being able to interpret signs. She gives some personal examples to illustrate her points.

'Spirit people always know who's there in the congregation, and it's often those who shout the loudest that get heard! Sometimes animals will appear, especially those that loved you and you loved them. On one occasion I saw an elephant standing next to a man. I thought this was rather silly and wasn't going to mention it, but in the end I did.

'It turned out the person I described was the father of a member of the church and that he'd been a circus entertainer who used an elephant as part of his act. If I'd decided to veto the impression, the opportunity to prove the existence of a relation in the spirit world, which is the medium's job, might have been lost. I had to trust what I was being shown.

'Having said that, if I haven't got a message right – and occasionally I don't – they'll keep bringing the image back. On another occasion I was describing a man who was holding a wine glass up in front of me. I interpreted this as meaning a celebration was on the horizon, as symbolism is commonly used in this way.

'So I duly told the lady in the congregation what I felt would be happening. But within a minute the man had brought the glass back again, and I had to return to the lady and ask her whether she knew anyone for whom a wine glass would have been significant. Yes, her husband had been a wine merchant! You have to bear in mind how difficult it can be for the spirit people – I don't always hear them and so they have to show me things which I then have to decipher as best I can...

'And even the best medium in the world can still come unstuck – although again, it's often a question of interpretation. About a year before my sister Linda died, she had a sitting with a medium whose credentials are the highest you could expect to find. She told Linda she could see her working as a secretary to a church and that she would become a member of the SNU's administrative district council. At the time Linda wasn't even a member of the church, but she was really excited by this lovely news and we chatted about it often.

'When Linda died suddenly twelve months later, I was already secretary of Wadebridge church and last June David and I were invited onto the SNU district council. Linda didn't actually do either of these things, a fact which perturbed me because I wondered how such a well-respected medium could have got things so wrong. It seemed that what she had seen was connected with me and not my sister.

'Being of a questioning nature and not accepting everything at face value, I asked another medium for her opinion. She wasn't at all surprised, suggesting that because we had such an extraordinary bond between us what was going on in my life would naturally show up in my sister's too. Now Linda's in the spirit world she works very closely with me, so she's actually playing a larger part in what we do than ever before. And in that respect the medium was exactly right!'

I quiz Janet on how she knows Linda is still around. Might it not be a case of wishing she was in contact with her? She agrees it could be construed like that, except: 'I've had messages from Linda from people who are practising their mediumship and they don't know either of us from Adam. They describe a woman in her early forties with long blond hair, a lively vivacious and dancing person – which is my sister to a T.

'Confirmation coming from others is more meaningful, because I challenge anything I feel might be just wishful thinking on my part.

'It's important for anybody to think carefully about a spirit's messages. Just because someone has died doesn't mean they've become a saint overnight or they suddenly have all the answers to everything! They continue to love you, but if they were a misery here, they'll be a misery over there! And if, say, someone was extremely prejudiced and they came through to advise a relative, that relative would have to remember those prejudices and not be swayed from doing what they themselves judge to be right. Personal responsibility has to come into it.'

Janet's and David's breadth of experience has now expanded beyond all expectations and their spiritual rewards, according to Janet, have been 'staggering'. But they both insist they are still learning and will continue to do so, especially through helping others develop. Janet is busy meeting rigorous demands to qualify as an assistant tutor, while David assesses course work for students training to be healers, an appropriate task to take on as his own healing gifts have flourished so spectacularly.

He recalls, without a hint of pride, a patient with cancer of the oesophagus and liver for whom doctors had run out of ideas. The healing energy David channelled enabled the man to live for a further fourteen months, during which time he saw another Christmas with his family, attended his son's wedding, and lost all fear of dying – and he could still enjoy tucking into steak and chips!

There was a knock-on effect too, as other cancer sufferers heard his story and also sought out David. All were assisted in some way, be it through gaining strength to endure chemo-therapy or making a full recovery. As David vouches, 'Healing comes from the world of Spirit and is channelled through the healer to the spirit of the other person, and will then work on whatever level is needed – not necessarily the physical.'

He chuckles when he is reminded of that night in the driving rain when his future was mapped out for him. There is no doubt about his healing, but what of his mediumship? So far he has only hinted at it. With a bit of prompting he quietly describes himself as a 'trance' medium, which sounds rather strange and so he explains further.

'It's a different sort of mediumship from Janet's. It's more passive – you allow a spirit to blend with you to the point where they control your body so that when you open your mouth the words you speak are their thoughts and not your own. But I'm not "taken over" and I don't lose consciousness – in fact my senses are heightened and I know what's going on around me.

'My mind is always in control: nothing happens unless I let it. I receive someone else's thoughts and words, which might not necessarily be my views, but a spirit is entitled to their own opinions, just as we are. So that's fine. But if, for example, they used language I didn't care for, I would say "No, I'm not going to say that!"'

According to David, the messages received in this way are generally answers to philosophical questions posed by members of their development circle which meets in private at their home: they have a beautiful, tranquil 'sanctuary' devoted specifically to spiritual work where pictures of their guides gaze down benignly from the walls.

Is this the church referred to by that canny medium almost ten years earlier? 'Perhaps!' David reflects, 'We certainly have all sorts of people visit us here to take part in our workshops, development circle, healing sessions and private consultations – from young single parents to 70+ year olds. It's so rewarding to watch them grow in confidence and begin to believe in themselves. But who knows what might happen in another ten years!'

Louise Hopkinson,
spiritual teacher and dream interpreter

A wind chime shivers in the cool breeze and back-combed clouds scud along friskily in front of an intense forget-me-not blue sky. At her porch awaits a slenderly built woman whose welcoming smile I imagine will chase away any furrow from a harassed brow.

I am greeted with a warm hug and ushered into an equally genial farmhouse kitchen where dried herbs are suspended above a large wooden table glowing with up-turned CD disks for mats. Sipping from steaming mugs of tea, we exchange pleasantries and are soon deep in conversation. We might have known each other for years.

For Louise Hopkinson, a school teacher by profession, every moment of every day is a spiritual experience from which to learn and move forwards. She speaks with such joyous author-ity you might be forgiven for thinking she has sailed through life without hitting any of the choppy waters most of us have to navigate from time to time. But this isn't the case at all; the only difference is that she views each potential obstacle as merely a challenge, a springboard to greater enlightenment. It would appear that after years of dedication very little, if at all, ruffles her luminescent feathers. Her mission now is to guide others to reach their own equanimity or, as she prefers to see it, to help them onto and along their spiritual path.

Our discussion kicks off with what in some circles is known as 'the spiritual wake-up call'. It could broadly be defined as a set of circumstances, usually uncomfortable, in a person's life which prompt them to take stock and start thinking seriously about spiritual matters.

Louise explains further: 'There seem to be three common ways people receive their wake-up call. The first can be when a family member or someone close to you dies, and you have to deal with physical separation and all the emotions attached to that. The second can come when your whole world is falling apart – you might have relationship problems, or you lose your job, or both. Cracks seem to open up everywhere. The third can happen when your life is moving at a fast pace and you're so involved with work you can't explore anything else, even though you want to. This often results in an illness and you're knocked out flat or bedridden. Time is then created for you.'

Louise's personal clarion call was not untypical. It came out of the blue when her mother was unexpectedly rushed into hospital with what the family thought was a bad bout of influenza. Tests soon revealed a brain tumour and the grim medical pronouncement was that Louise's mother had just twenty-four hours to live. As it turned out, she beat the doctors' prediction, but ultimately was unable to defeat the cancer and two months later she died.

While organising the funeral arrangements, Louise's father made a special request that she should pay her respects to her mother by visiting the undertaker's and viewing the body in the coffin. She recalls, 'This was the last thing on my mind. I had never come across this sort of situation before and I had no desire to see a dead body.' But not wishing to offend her father, she obediently went along to what she describes as 'that cold, unfriendly room' where staff wheeled out her mother 'dressed in that most peculiar way they dress deceased people'.

She was drawn to look at her mother's long, tapering fingers and casually remarked to herself in a half-joking, though not disrespectful, fashion that a lifelong desire to have elegant hands had been granted. Gone were the square, stocky digits, but also gone were the generous feminine curves elsewhere – it took only a few seconds for Louise to widen her gaze and acknowledge the sombre effects of the ravaging disease.

Rather than feeling sad or upset, however, Louise admits she was relieved. She instantly grasped that, although she was look-ing at a body, the real 'essence' of her mother was no longer there. The realisation was comforting, and it also marked a crucial turning point by forcing her to ask, 'If she's not here, where is she?'

In a vague way she probably already knew. During the next week and particularly at the funeral and cremation while watching the coffin disappear behind the thick velvet curtains, she sensed a presence standing behind her, surveying the proceedings, which filled her with an inner excitement.

Returning home, she borrowed books from the local library in the hope she would find a rational answer to her question. Like many people exposed to grief for the first time, she was attracted by the idea of spirits residing in another place after death. Through her reading she came across stories of clairvoyants providing indisputable evidence – nicknames, intimate family incidents and private jokes – to bereaved folk, and of near-death experiences which had so many uncanny similarities with each other that the odds of there being a common strand to all seemed very great.

Finally, an evening witnessing at close hand the skills of the internationally famous Doris Stokes convinced her beyond any doubt of some form of life after death. As the medium established a connection between this world and the next, and conveyed one affecting message after another, gasps of amazement and joy among the audience were profoundly moving. Louise was deeply impressed, and at last content that the first piece in her intricate jigsaw had been slotted into place.

However, with such an enquiring mind, she could not rest there for long. If convincing accounts of pastlife regressions had any credence, had her mother, if not the whole family, gone through similar scenarios countless times before? And if so, why?

Over the years her search for explanations has yielded nuggets of pure gold so that today her responses to similar queries are spoken with unshakable confidence: 'Because of what I have learned spiritually, I now know this other side or the place where your essence – the real you or your soul – goes when you pass over is called the fourth dimension. Some refer to it as the spirit world.

'There are, in fact, many dimensions (thirteen altogether) existing in one space which lead back to the creator, God, Source, All That Is, or whatever else you want to call where we came from in the beginning. The easiest way I describe it is to use the analogy of tuning in to stations and channels on radio and television. We know they're all out there, it's just a matter of adjusting the dials and selecting the right one.

'Spiritually speaking, we can pick up signs coming from another station or dimension by harmonising with the frequencies. Sometimes this ability is passed on through generations in one family – mediums will often say their grandmother was clairvoyant – but in most instances it's down to individuals working on themselves and opening their minds up to a bank of new knowledge.

'It's very much about starting to raise your awareness or, to use one of my favourite phrases, "doing the sponge act" – you're curious about everything and you seek out books or tapes, and you attend courses and lectures. Once you've begun establishing what feels right for you, your own truth, you're well on your way to accessing new possibilities.'

One last comment about reincarnation completes the picture: 'When you've experienced one dimension from every perspective, you can then choose to move on to the next. At the moment we're in the third and until we've learned all we need to from this physical plane we'll keep coming back. When we die, our soul passes over into the fourth dimension, but after a rest and a review of our most recent life for many it's then back to earth with a bump!'

Louise confirms that not everybody races ahead after their wake-up call at the same speed. For her, the responsibilities of caring for two young children took precedence once the family had resumed its normal routines after the funeral. Her initial investigative flurry soon dwindled and metaphysical issues were put on hold. She has since watched others experience similar stops and starts: 'It's as though we open the door a little bit, and then realise it's not time to open it fully. We don't forget what we've learned, but we may go a year or several before we push against it some more.'

Here Louise introduces another useful metaphor: 'Making a spiritual journey is like stepping on and off a moving pavement. At the start it's exciting when you're dipping into fresh subjects, and you're going along at a fair old rate. Then you discover that for every question you find an answer to there are a hundred more needing a solution.

'At this stage people can feel overwhelmed, and decide to pause or get on with the rest of their life, perhaps chewing over snippets of knowledge every now and then. They choose to step off the moving pavement, because it's not appropriate for them to go any further just yet, and that's fine – there is no right or wrong, only what is perfect for each person at any moment.

'It's also true to say that if you're thoroughly involved in your physical existence – earning a living, paying the bills – your spiritual side has to take a step backwards. You have to deal with these issues first before you can dedicate yourself totally to your spiritual service. With the best will in the world, if you're worried about whether you can feed the family, you can't be thinking on a higher plane about where the angels fit into your life!'

We turn to 1987, to the gales that ravaged the landscape across the country and to a pivotal decision made while leaning into the violent wind and registering the shocking scenes of natural destruction. Louise collects her thoughts. Before she resumes this next chapter of her story, she prefaces it with an episode from only a few weeks ago when a lady raised an intriguing topic during an evening class.

Having analysed her life after a prolonged illness, she wished to know whether 'your soul ever speaks to you'. The rest of the group were amused by her quirky line of thinking, but Louise

seized on the opportunity to explore the notion in her characteristically insightful way. Her response was refreshingly candid: 'I believe it can, but it doesn't use words – it speaks by way of a feeling which is so strong you cannot deny it even if your brain is telling you it's absolute rubbish! Once your soul speaks, that's it – you have to listen.'

I begin to appreciate why the events Louise organises are so popular: her warm northern tones are familiar and comfortable; her down to earth phrases are gently thought-provoking and impart a subtle understanding of the human condition and how to rise above its apparent limitations. She now relates how her own soul spoke forcibly, generating an irresistible urge to move to the West Country and press further along her spiritual path.

She flips quickly back to the late 1970s. The family spent a couple of holidays 'of sheer bliss and enjoyment' in Cornwall – a place she and husband Andy soon prized as the most natural for them to be. As they drove home after the second trip, Louise is not embarrassed to admit she was devastated by feelings of loss and separation. Tears were still pouring down her cheeks as they travelled along the Embankment in London. She and Andy then made a pact that one day they would live in the south west.

She fast forwards ten years to the autumn of 1987 when Essex was subjected to a crushing hurricane. The youngest member of the Hopkinson household requested in childish innocence that his parents 'Please turn the wind down!' As the sun rose among blood-red clouds after the night of greatest destruction, they were utterly dismayed to see electricity cables flailing wildly in the air, cars spun onto their roofs like helpless upturned beetles, and trees carelessly spilled on the earth – including those from their own cherished garden – as though shaken from a box of matches. What had been a leafy conurbation had metamorphosed into a grey network of concrete and brick.

The enormity of the catastrophe compelled Louise finally to address an apprehension that had long been fermenting. She was unhappy with the community's materialistic fixations: 'I didn't want the children to get any older in an area which was so focused on not who you were but how much you earned, what your latest car was and where you were going on holiday. I didn't wish to play that game any more. It seemed the time was right for the big move.'

She continues: 'I have since discovered that once you put out a call or a request to the universe it really is a case of "Ask and you shall receive". Within a week, some friends came over one evening full of excitement. They had been to Cornwall and out of curiosity had compared house prices. The difference between the two areas was considerable, Essex at that time being much more expensive. It was then that my soul not only spoke, it leapt! It seemed the dream we'd had at the back of our minds for so long could become a reality.'

They decided to take a gamble and risk moving without finding a secure job first. There would be enough money to buy a house and, if they economised, a little left over to see them through the next year. They sensed an urgency to commit themselves swiftly and the reason soon became clear: the rules on tax relief were to change shortly which, as it transpired, resulted in the housing market coming to a standstill and prices in Cornwall rising.

It began to look as if their uprooting was indeed divinely willed. Louise's reaction to this inference is startling: 'In spiritual circles the hurricane of 1987 is known as "the winds of change". I can sum it up in very simple terms: higher dimensional beings overseeing our spiritual development had discerned that, although a lot of people were already on the path, many others needed a nudge in the right direction. As a consequence, the "harmonic convergence" in August that year (when hundreds of thousands of people all over the world focused on peace) brought about a huge inpouring of energy that subsequently affected individuals in different ways.

'This might sound like a contradiction in terms, but I believe that help for me came through the devastation wrought by the hurricane. Whatever happens in life always has two interpretations: the physical and the spiritual – the two have to go hand in hand. It was no coincidence – because there are no coincidences! – that I felt this tug of my soul at what in hindsight was a momentous turning point in my life. There were also many, many other people of like-mind drawn to Cornwall for spiritual reasons at exactly the same time, and the trend continues.'

The transition was not easy. Last-minute hitches meant that the asking price of the home they had chosen in a small hamlet outside Bude was suddenly raised.

Louise looks back on the difficult situation with some amusement: 'We all have our spiritual challenges or, as I like to call them, end of term tests, to see how well we're doing. We had to make the decision to dip into our pot and pay the extra cash or start looking for another house.

Three o'clock one night I shot bolt upright in bed and said, "We've got to let go of the money – it's all part of the challenge!" And that's how we ended up here in 1988 facing a new life with hardly any finances!'

As the main breadwinner in the family, Louise concedes that while she was driving all over the county as a supply teacher she couldn't make the spiritual commitment she would have liked. It had to wait until she was settled in a full-time teaching post and their monetary problems were easing. Then, the bells resumed their pealing.

One evening, on impulse, she and Andy ventured out for a walk. No sooner had they meandered a few hundred metres down the road when their attention was caught by a notice in the front window of a bungalow, only three houses down from their own. They took a sizable pace back in amazement, and re-read the small advertisement which invited anyone interested in a new spiritualist church to attend a forthcoming meeting.

They never finished their stroll, but turned straight around and launched into conversation about what would be involved. The next day Louise even asked the religious education teacher at school for her opinion, because she thought she needed as much information beforehand as she could gather.

Now she believes otherwise: 'That was very much the mental part of me telling me I didn't need to bother going as I had quite enough on my plate with school work. But my soul was jumping up and down, saying "Come on, this is a sign!" There's a wonderful phrase the writer and healer Denise Linn uses, "the universe is whispering to you", which describes rather poetically how there are hundreds of signs all about us every day. It's whether we become aware of them and acknowledge their significance that's important. In my case I'd missed an ad in the local newspaper, so I had to go on a walk for another sign to be pointed out.'

Louise listened to her inner voice and went to the meeting. The organisers had recently moved to Bude and were greatly motivated to found a church because of the enormous amount of help they had received from mediums after the man's son was tragically killed in a motorbike accident.

Not only was it agreed the project should go ahead, but Louise was allocated the job of treasurer. She recalls: 'By the end of the evening there was so much *enthusiasm* – and I use the word purposefully, as its correct definition means linking with your spirit or soul. I have no doubt in saying that when we feel completely energised and enthused by something, it's because we're following our soul's next stage of development. It's evidence, if you like, that we're on the right track.'

With Andy's unstinting support, Louise offered their cosy kitchen as a venue for the weekly development circle, although she wasn't sure exactly what part she would play. She had accepted early on that she was not cut out to be a conventional hands-on healer, and she had no wish to be a platform medium 'to bring Aunt Bertha through'. But she kept an open mind, and gradually her role became more defined.

Every meeting began with a meditation. For those who were training, it was a quiet period to meet up with their guides and receive information. Not everybody felt satisfied afterwards however: some could not understand the images they had seen, while others dismissed the exercise if they had not heard words spoken. Always believing the meditations held important keys for the participants, Louise helped overcome frustrations by adopting a positive attitude.

Instead of ignoring seemingly obscure symbols, she set about interpreting them in the light of each person's physical situation, their health, their work and their relationships. She followed a strong inner feeling and, assisted by feedback from group members, developed an expertise which provided the elusive 'purpose' to her involvement she had been seeking.

From here it was a short hop to dream interpretation. Louise readily confesses that, since she leads a busy life and has an active mind, she does not find meditation easy. But she realised that if people could derive so much benefit from it, there must be another way for others to tap into the same spiritual guidance which she believes is open to all.

'It shouldn't be a case of, hard luck, you can't get this knowledge because you don't meditate!', she quips, 'I thought about how else we receive images in a literal or symbolic form. What leapt straight to mind was dreaming. Everyone has dreams, whether they remember them or not.

'Apparently the Romans and the Greeks used to have a dream interpretation session at breakfast every morning, and some native cultures still call it the "dream time". Recently I was interested to hear a top psychologist on Radio 4 expressing concern about people leading such hectic lives they don't have time to analyse their dreams. He was referring particularly to those in stress-related jobs who never stop thinking about work. While he acknowledged it would be good business for him in the future, on a more considerate level he suggested that not attending to what's cropping up now in dreams will build problems for the future. So he's set up a web site, hoping this will be a good way of communicating with those most at risk.'

At the outset Louise used her own dreams to hone her interpretation skills, on the assumption it is best to become confident with yourself and your own abilities before involving other people. She recognised so many meaningful personal messages that it was not long before she came to the conclusion 'dreams are not just a random series of events that happen when we're asleep'. She also rapidly dispensed with the old belief that if she could recall her nocturnal visions, she hadn't slept well! Now she advises friends to ask for guidance during the night by phrasing a suitable question in their head before going to sleep or by writing it on paper and slipping it under the pillow.

She distinguished different types of dream too, including those with especial significance: 'I refer to these as the "big ones" or the "whammy ones" where when you wake up you know you've had a spiritual experience.' She shares one of these with me to demonstrate how powerful dreams can motivate those brave enough to extricate themselves from stultifying dilemmas.

This particular dream arrived when Louise was debating with herself about whether, after two years, she should break from the spiritualist church. She had commitments every night of the week and often at weekends too and was perplexed at not being able to pursue other spiritual tacks. At the same time, she felt a responsibility to development circle members who used her house for meetings. The conflicting issues were dominating her subconscious.

She sketches out her dream: 'I was helping people get into boats so they could all leave an island safely. Then I noticed that everybody had already left – they were just a speck in the distance – and I'd missed the last ferry. So although everything was in symbols, to me it meant that if I wasn't careful I really would "miss the boat". I was putting everybody else first and wasn't considering my own spiritual development – or evolution of my soul as I now call it.'

Bolstered by this intelligence, Louise bravely faced the group, expecting dismay and outrage. Instead, as often happens when fears are faced head on, there was relief as all agreed the forum had run its course but they hadn't had the courage to raise the item for debate.

Once that hurdle was cleared Louise was free to move on, though as yet she did not know in which direction. Her inspiration soon arrived while she was enjoying one of her own preferred methods of meditation – a nice hot bath! She laughs: 'I was filled with such excitement I sprang out of the water and rushed, dripping, to share it with Andy.

'I knew I had to start an awareness group where we could look at mind, body and spirit issues. It would involve speakers, discussions, meditation, books, tapes, complementary therapists and a general sharing of ideas and experiences. I even got the name "Mandala" whilst in the bath – a mandala is a sort of symbolic circular figure which represents the universe and completeness.'

The word was duly spread around and on its first night Mandala attracted eight people. The next week there were eighteen, and since then over three hundred people have passed through Andy's and Louise's front door. Ever mindful of a broad range of needs, Louise has branched out to run regular courses and workshops at weekends as well.

'Soon after we started Mandala,' she says, 'it became obvious that some people who come along are very much just setting out on their spiritual paths. They have questions that can't always be answered within the limits of a Monday evening. So I now have one- and two-day courses on related themes – auras and chakras, our spiritual helpers, the choices our soul makes, the ascended masters (beings or energies in the higher dimensions), dream interpretation etc.

'I also offer sessions for personal growth and development which help people let go of problems they may have been hanging onto since childhood – something I've had to work on myself, so I empathise with what others are going through.'

Louise remains thankful for her twenty-five years as a teacher: 'Sometimes the secret to finding out your spiritual "mission" is to look inwards and see what talents you already have rather than feeling you have to learn new skills. I'm used to gathering information, presenting it in an interesting way, standing up in front of people, and that sort of thing. So my day job, and I use the word "job" deliberately, has equipped me well for my spiritual work.'

This 'work' impels her continually to think laterally about how to reach an ever widening audience. Unlikely routes such as adult education courses on spiritual awareness, for example, have drawn in people who would not necessarily discover Mandala. And then there's the intriguingly named 'Transformation Game'.

Louise explains, 'It's a board game originally devised at the Findhorn spiritual community in Scotland. The idea is that you bring an issue with you that you want to explore, and as the game progresses every move is interpreted with that in mind. Some people will just think oh, it's a board game so it can't help me spiritually, but as facilitator I can vouch it provides amazing revelations!'

I wonder what else Louise has up her sleeve. Where is her unboundless energy taking her?

She answers ebulliently: 'Although over the years my time management has become extremely good, I'm aware there are still occasions when I do a seven-day week – teaching, marking books, weekend courses and fairs, and trying to fit the washing in! During the last summer holiday feedback from an experimental day's course in Essex was so encouraging that I'm taking the plunge and going part-time at school. This will give me a better balance – I'll have two extra days a week to devote to spiritual activities, perhaps travelling further afield and offering a wider choice of courses. The signs are quite definite. This is the next step I must take.'

I am struck by this remarkable woman's wisdom and charisma and equally admiring of her husband's supportive strength of character. I leave with a flurry of sage words impressing on my mind: 'There is no one route to spiritual enlightenment. Each person is following their own path, doing their own thing, and no one is better than anyone else – remember the maxim: "If there was only meant to be one way, there'd only be a need for one person!"'

And finally, in typically uplifting vein: 'Once you've made that connection with your soul, the real you, then life can never be the same again. I feel it's incredibly exciting and just a wonderful adventure!'

Patrick Gamble,
spiritually-inspired artist

Patrick Gamble is tall and slim, with a beautiful lilting voice. His cadences rise and fall, ebb and flow as he chooses words carefully. Their texture reflects a life seasoned by travel – from Devon to Australia, to South Africa and Zimbabwe, and then back to the West Country, to Cornwall where he 'just came and stayed'. He has no immediate plans to leave, but is simply enjoying being here.

We chat for a few minutes until I am jolted away from my train of thought. Behind him, hanging in the corner of a room in his neat and homely cottage, is a remarkable painting – of an angel, a dazzlingly vibrant being with striking facial features, luxuriant black hair surging down to powerful shoulders, and wings lustrous as golden eagle feathers burnished by a Mediterranean mid-day sun.

This unforgettable image is just one of many Patrick has painted after it was revealed to him by 'Spirit', something he defines as 'a movement of another reality', adding, 'We all may give it different names, but it doesn't really matter.'

I turn back from admiring the angel and notice a couple of deep red notches cut into Patrick's knuckles as he raises his hands to direct me towards a chair. It hits home to me that these scuffs are not paint smudges, as I might have expected, but the hallmarks of the building trade from which he earns his living. At heart he is a 'practical, nuts and bolts man' who used to be an atheist and was more at ease with a chisel and a hammer than with a delicate paint brush. But one dramatic afternoon ten years ago the status quo was irrevocably altered.

A colleague was moving away and he asked Patrick if he would take a box of odds and ends. No one else was interested and so, according to Patrick, the dusty old container ended up on his doorstep. Not knowing what to do with it, he carried it into his garage and left it there. Several weeks later he woke up in determined mood, and decided to tidy the garage and haul what he didn't need to the tip. Instead of setting to and clearing all the accumulated debris, he found himself looking into the box. He says, 'I knew there was a canvas in there, and I think there were three tubes of paint. I went back up to the house to do a bit of abstract dawbing as a joke for my wife. I can remember standing the canvas up, and that's about it.'

What Patrick describes next usually has people riveted to their seats: 'Two hours later I came around, covered in paint. I was on the kitchen floor, sobbing. I looked up and there was a man's face on the canvas. I can't recall painting him, and I actually thought there was someone else in the house who'd done it – though I thought lots of things, maybe that I was going off my head! It was all very emotional. I knew something had started, that my heart had been touched, but I didn't realise there would be more to follow.'

As the months went by other peculiar incidents did take place – flickers or shadows drifting past windows, strange dreams, and glimpses of things which disappeared as soon as he looked in their direction. However, it was the picture which focused his attention the most.

Slowly but surely he realised he had to come to terms with the fact it was he who had portrayed the man's face and that, for some reason unknown to him, he was the recipient of a wondrous spiritual gift. He began to understand, too, that he should develop his newly acquired skills not only for himself, but for others. And so he allowed them to gather momentum, though he never again painted without consciously being aware of his actions.

As happens now, he was 'shown' images which he then captured in oils. In those early days these seemed to be part of his own spiritual education, rather as the pictures on tarot cards hint at a person's destiny. He is of the opinion that he was being given clues to what had 'made me into an unbeliever'.

There is a hush as he pauses fleetingly to unwrap the next sheaf of thoughts. Then he carries on, quietly, phrases rippling across the still pool created by his eloquent silences: 'I was being shown, I guess, why I'd gone through life's experiences…how we have all chosen to come here…how we pick our parents, our soul fills our physical being and then we start to live our life.

'We need each other and we're here to teach each other. The experiences along the way are our teachers as well, although even now, ten years later, it doesn't get any easier! I think once you're aware of Spirit in some ways it makes it harder.

'I also believe each of us has a gift or an ability. Sometimes it's hard to find, or maybe it's staring us in the face and other people can see it! We need to keep trusting, something I still find difficult. I still am learning, and it goes on…'

Since those early days Patrick has discovered how to 'control' his incredible talent so that it no longer impinges on areas of his life he prefers to keep separate. He elaborates: 'I had to be careful, because it was affecting my job… and it was affecting me… So I had to learn how to work with the energies, how to open and to shut down. That's why for me, physical tasks are important – they ground me, keep me in reality. I'm not one of those people who can work with Spirit all the time. I would become too disconnected.'

Paintings, apparently, can start and be completed in any number of ways. Sometimes he hears a loud whisper calling his name, while at other times he simply feels it would be appropriate to unwrap a canvas. So this is just what he does – he leans a new panel against the wall, its pristine surface looking stern yet vulnerable, and waits what might be a few minutes or hours, or maybe several weeks.

There are also instances when, to put it rather simplistically, a message arrives while he's dreaming. As soon as this happens he immediately gets up from his bed, whatever time of night that may be, and begins painting. He says: 'It could be just colour that is laid down that first night or there may be images which are rapidly put down. Or I might paint one tiny bit in the corner, even though the canvas could be six feet tall. And then I perhaps wait a week. Or I might paint through the night and continue on the next day – it can be that strong.'

Patrick offers me a selection of blank greetings cards as further examples of his 'work with Spirit'. Each has a different, small reproduction of one of his magnificent pictures. I study an old man's face, wispy white hair fluttering to the breath of iridescent butterflies' wings which beat in violet mist about his head. A sparkling crystal ball placed delicately on the fingertips of his right hand looks both solid and ethereal. It takes a few minutes for me to register the conceit in the fabrication of his subtly patterned garment, and then I smile to myself. His right shoulder is enveloped by the upper wing of an enormous butterfly, while the scalloped-edged robe hanging from his elbow is formed from its lower gossamer wing.

I choose another card. Top right and bottom, swirling areas of emerald green and midnight blue are splashed with sea spray and the hinted outline of a dolphin dives downwards. In the centre, ebony eyes set in a strong native American face steadily hold my gaze. Fronds of black hair are swept outwards, merging with the thick fur of three wolves who, each in different pose, tenderly nuzzle their heads into the young man's.

My third choice again makes a connection between the raw beauty of the natural world and the mystical realms. It is dominated by the head and neck of a bird of prey, dark brown and fawn feathers bristling with energy. The majestic creature's beak is hooked around a large golden ring that spins like a glowing Catherine wheel and shoots out scatters of sequinned star dust.

Now seems a suitable point for Patrick to clarify how he manages to paint such magical scenes when he has had no formal art training – ever. He divulges that he has three guides, one of whom called John he believes plays a large part in the creative process.

Although he has scant details about John's background, it is obvious from Patrick's expression that he enjoys a warm relationship with him which he says has been a great support over the years: 'John was born in London in the 1800s and lived to the age of about 40. He had bad health and struggled as an artist, and he was very spiritually aware, but back then you couldn't show it. Apart from that, I don't know much about him. I don't even know that I'll see any of his work, and I've never painted him.' As an aside and gently stressing each syllable, he adds, 'He will not be painted, though I live in hope...'

Patrick confirms that if he attempted to paint without John's help, without tuning in through an opening prayer, the results would be less than pretty! I enquire whether John is always around and Patrick implies that he is. But then he decides to amplify his statement a little by reporting, 'When I say always, he's not let me down. But there will be times when he "goes away"... or perhaps he doesn't go away as such, but lets me get on with other things – which is probably more to the point.

'I've had two periods of six months when I couldn't paint. I tried, and got everything ready and even put paint on the canvas, but it turned to what I call mud. This can sometimes happen if I'm in front of other people...' I commiserate and express concern on his behalf, but he continues steadily, 'These things happen. It lets me know that I am just a link within a chain. The painting is not mine in that respect.'

Patrick is often to be found at 'mind, body and spirit' events where he likes to position himself in a secluded corner, art board on his knee, paintbrush in his hand, and tubes of pigments spread within easy reaching distance. He looks up frequently, glancing about a metre above his sitters' heads and rarely at them directly. He paints steadily throughout the day, with barely a minute to himself as he captures the fabulous images he sees around each person.

Dealing with individuals and the energies surrounding them in this way took Patrick around four or five years to master. It is now one of the most rewarding aspects of his painting, as he is able to furnish people with very special pieces of artwork whose meaningful symbols and messages are specific to them. He says, 'Most of my work seems to show guides, although it has to be said that the number of family members and loved ones has increased in the last twelve months.'

However, he can never guarantee the results of a sitting: 'Sometimes the images shown to me aren't very strong or they don't last, or sometimes there's nothing apart from colour. One day a lady came and all I could see around her was pink in many different tones. I laid these down on the board and at the end that's all I could give her – there was nothing else... As it turned out, this lady had lost her husband and so, although it would have been nice to paint her husband, it was the pink of love that was enveloping her at that time. Colour is medicine, a tonic, and something we all need. I once saw a painting a blind man had done to music. He could actually feel the harmonies and that showed me how you can pick up on vibrations of colour.'

Patrick acknowledges it can be quite difficult both for him and for his clients when expectations are not met: 'Sometimes people really need a message from a loved one and it just isn't there. I remember a man phoning me and asking if he could bring his wife, as their son had recently died. I explained that what they were hoping for might not happen, but he insisted... They duly arrived, and her son didn't come.'

He takes several measured breaths and then says, 'I knew that that probably would be the case. But there again, another lady visited me, said nothing, and she did have her son painted. That's the way it is, so I don't question any more.' Then, in almost a whisper, he confesses, 'It is odd. I do understand... but I don't always understand...'

Patrick's occasional admissions of human frailty and his empathy with fellow travellers careering into the potholes along life's unmade roads are extremely touching. He sits back in his chair. I follow his movements and as I do so my eyes are drawn upwards. There, standing sideways on to the room, with his face turned to look over his right shoulder, is another angel. Again, I am caught unawares, and once again, I'm hugely impressed by a picture's boldness and unconventionality – the exotic winged figure, most surprisingly, has a smooth head and unusually shaped ears. I feel a tremor of excitement, an air of expectation. I keep watching.

The angel's demeanour becomes as soft as rippling fields of corn blown by summer breezes, and then as intense as a cascading waterfall. Patrick casually observes: 'The angel paintings came about for the millennium – there seems to be increased activity among the angels as part of the healing of the planet. The two I've painted are around...' He leaves it at that, and it doesn't seem the right moment to press for any more information.

Instead, I shuffle a few more cards on my lap and welcome the hush to absorb a new image, that of a white-headed eagle among whose lower feathers shelter the faintly suggested shapes of a wolf and a bear. I glean from Patrick that the painting originated during a period in his life when he needed the fortitude that this noble creature represents. He says, 'The paintings are my teachers, but they are also there to help other people. The energy of that eagle is very very strong. If you connect with it, you will be filled with the medicine of courage and strength, and you'll be able to look down and see not only yourself but what's around you as well...'

I catch a vague waft of linseed oil. I hear from Patrick that he keeps his paints and boards and so on in the adjoining room where visitors sit for up to an hour for their picture. Days or weeks afterwards people often tell him the colours have changed, becoming lighter or brighter.

Opposite: The eagle was painted at a time in Patrick's life when he needed the strength of this majestic creature and its connection with 'the Great Spirit'

He explains this phenomenon: 'Although the pictures have been brought through into a physical medium, they are still a form of energy, and they give and take. They can create a shift in your life too. I'm only now beginning to be aware of all these things… how time doesn't exist for them, for Spirit, but it does for us, and how everything will happen… you just can't rush it!'

Another faint draught brings the comforting aroma of the flaxen oil, and we revisit the subject of spiritual guides one last time. I ask Patrick for his opinion in a nutshell. His reply is a fitting conclusion to this book: 'I feel the benefits which our spiritual guides bring are incalculable. With our family and loved ones, we have an emotional attachment and we are linked through our physical-ness. But a spiritual connection goes much beyond that. Our guides are here to help us bring about change within ourselves and in this world…'

Note

If you would like to contact any of the people featured in *Spiritual Guides in the West Country*, please write to them c/o the publishers, Bossiney Books. Alternatively, you can visit websites for more information or get in touch via e-mail:

Neil Beechwood, e-mail: neil.beechwood@ntlworld.com

Martin Cox, e-mail: martincox60@hotmail.com

Stephen Cox, e-mail: steve.cox18@virgin.net

Patrick Gamble, e-mail: patrickgamble@totalise.co
  website: http://patrickgamble.co-uk.to

David Gay, e-mail: davidgay@rescorla.fsnet.co.uk
  website: www.webspawner.com/users/djmediumsunlimited
Louise Hopkinson, website: www.geocities.com/mandalagroup
Lynne Orchard, Chalice Well website:www.chalicewell.org.uk
Thomas, e-mail: thomas.j.gribble@btinternet.com